The Heart in Communicating

One person's journey from broadcaster to crisis communicator

By
Richard Brundage

Best Wishes

Dick Bruaford
2007

The Heart in Communicating

Dedicated to my father and mother,

Walter and Christine Brundage, who gave me a great sense of history, not only of the Brundage family,

but the stewardship we all have in passing on our own family histories while developing our place in them.

"We are not permitted to choose the frame of our destiny. But what we put into it is ours".

Dag Hammarskjold

The Heart in Communicating

FIRST THOUGHTS   3/24/2002

I guess my first thoughts are 'long overdue'. And since they are, I've taken the time to write this over several years.   My intent was not to create a compendium of random thoughts and anecdotes, but rather a collection of experiences and a blend of stories that will let the reader arrive at the main teaching points, and just maybe, have some fun along the way.

There are so many to thank and I would have to start with the participants in my seminars over the past 25 years. They've constantly asked me to write a book and put the stories and teaching points I tell in my live seminars down in writing. They've also added more content to this book than they know, and I'm constantly learning from them in every seminar I present. I think I've also become laser focused in the past decade on my seminar.

For me, writing this book became a passionate ministry, transferring to my many students, friends and professional associates in many occupations around the world the game plan for good public and media appearances and a return to communicating from the heart - something we did so well as children.

And beyond that, perhaps helping others I've yet to meet discover or recapture their own passionate commitment to their occupations or professions and the way they communicate those feelings to others. The bottom line to effective communications, especially in crisis events is to speak from the heart – not the head.

I hope this book will, above all, transcend just talking about media response training, or crisis/risk communications and actually move people to communicate better in a variety of situations, from public appearances, business interactions and in private family conversations.

There are those I will talk about in this book who have caused me to think about things in a different light, and some who became mentors, providing those personal epiphanies I'll share along the way, and whose contributions were never fully revealed to me at the time.

In some cases I only realized how important their words and actions were long after they were gone, as if there existed the need to incubate their contributions within my own frame of reference and experiences before finding the connection to a teaching point in my seminars or my own personal life.

For all of them, I'm grateful. For without those experiences in life we are all unable to grow, but with them we can realize just what it is we are supposed to contribute in this life.

I've attempted to make each chapter in this book a story, from which there are teaching points, some obvious and some that will cause the reader to pause and contemplate the meaning in context with their own life experiences.

Perhaps, from the earliest times, that's how we learned the best, through the stories that we passed to each other around campfires - information on life from one generation to the other. And today, a well told story still remains the most powerful and poignant communication tool.

And finally, I'm not an academician, so this approach to writing more closely resembles the way I teach - from the heart. Most of all, I hope you just sit back and enjoy one person's journey.

"Never apologize for showing feelings.
When you do so, you apologize for the truth"

Benjamin Disraeli

$(1804 - 1881)$

FORWARD

I had no intention whatsoever of writing a book, or for that matter of teaching risk and crisis communications and media response seminars around the world when in my early career years.

I thought I was moderately happy simply being in broadcasting, both radio and television and owning my own video production company.

Early in 1980, the television crew and I had flown all the way from Washington, D.C. - where I was the chief correspondent and occasional anchor for a program that appeared nationally on PBS, called "Small Business Journal" - to Anchorage, Alaska. It was quite a long trip, and actually the beginning of the rest of my life, although I didn't know it at the time.

My reason for going there was to interview the person who was selected as the Small Business Person of the Year, and produce a feature on him for my television program. Although I cannot remember this person's name, he was a very competent business owner and seemed easy to talk to until, of course, the crew turned on the lights, clipped on a microphone and pointed a camera at him.

It was a sit-down interview, which in his case was a terrible mistake. His coat was buttoned. Try never to button your coat if you're sitting down for an interview that is going to be filmed or taped. They don't hang well on the body that way.

I couldn't concentrate on much of what this fellow was saying, because I kept watching his coat leave his body. Literally. He also had 'photo-grey' glasses. You know, the kind that change from clear to dark when light hits them. And there was a lot of light on him and yes, his glasses got darker by the minute.

He also had 'closed' body language. Arms crossed, a body language signal that says the person is not going to volunteer any information. He would sometimes look to heaven for an answer to a question, and occasionally got the 'deer in the headlights' look when I would ask him a question he didn't think I would ask.

Even though this was going to be a very positive feature, and he was going to be seen by several million television viewers as the epitome of how to succeed in business, he exhibited all the visual attributes of a felon.

About 5 minutes into the interview, realizing that I could no longer see his eyes behind the now totally dark glasses, and with sweat running down his nose and cheeks, (try never to sweat on television; sweating is guilty - just don't do it.) I told the cameraman to shut off the camera, and asked the crew to turn out the lights and leave "Mr. Business Person of the Year" and me alone for a little while.

No one ever really knows when they are going to have a personal epiphany, but it was clear to me a few days later that I had just had one. I was about to cross the line from journalist to teacher.

I said to him, "I simply can't go back to Washington with a story like this. You look like you belong in jail, not on television in a positive business story. Look, let me show you some things that make me feel comfortable in front of a camera."

I never felt totally comfortable in front of a camera. Who does? No matter how much on-camera television I did I was always aware of that artificial environment: the camera, lights, crew, teleprompters, listening to the producer or director in one ear and trying to read and talk at the same time. It's simply not natural.

Anyway, I unloaded on this hapless creature, and for about 20 minutes or so I taught him a host of things that worked for me throughout the years. Things that made me relax and therefore communicate better.

I suppose in retrospect I may have been looking for a vessel to dump this knowledge into, or maybe I was looking for affirmation in another person that we're all on a stage every day, and acting is part of our daily lives, especially when you're on television.

If anyone tells you that being on television is not acting - they're crazy. In fact, the longer I stood in front of a camera doing stand ups, looking down the barrel of a camera, the more I felt like whatever I was saying was making absolutely no sense whatsoever!

You simply get no feedback from a camera like you do from a live audience. The camera just sits on the tripod silently with the red tally light blinking.

Well, for whatever the reasons, apparently I was very passionate about relaying my convictions to "Mr. Business Person of the Year" that day in Anchorage.

When I finished with my oral précis, I called the crew back in, plugged in the lights, turned on the camera and began anew my interview with this now very positive looking and passionately committed businessman.

The interview was a success. He looked great, sounded confident, smiled and generally took on the persona of a successful businessperson - which in truth he actually was. He had just re-learned how to communicate it all over again.

I thanked him for not only being patient, but for letting me unload all this information on him. Contrary to being offended, he was jubilant. He asked me if I could remain one extra day in Anchorage, and said, "If I get the community leaders together, could you teach us all how to do this?"

Before thinking, I said, "Yes". The personal epiphany was taking shape. I stayed up most of the night in my hotel room with a legal pad, putting academic handles on things that I instinctively knew, because, academically I never studied journalism.

In fact, my college degree was in biological science. So, what I was writing that night was not some academic treatise, but thoughts and formulas for successful communications on television, radio and in print.

The seminar the next day was pretty successful according to the feedback from the audience. I thought it was unstructured and a bit basic. And believe me it was. But, to my audience of community leaders it evidently contained some things they hadn't heard before. For me it was one of the most satisfying experiences of my life. I had become a teacher. If you have ever taught anything you know exactly what I mean.

In the several decades that have now passed since that day in Anchorage, I've refined, updated, refreshed, and added to a seminar that now is truly about "how" we say something, not so much "what" we say when we communicate.

I have never advertised my seminar, and yet it has taken me literally around the world - several times.

I've had the great fortune of teaching at the highest levels of government, military, business and industry. From U.S. Ambassadors at the State Department, Special Agents In Charge of guarding heads of state, to school superintendents and local public health officials trying to get a handle on crisis events.

And, nearly everyone I've taught has given me something back in return. I often say to my students, "I may learn more from you today than you learn from me." And, it's true.

I take their stories and experiences with me, and some of them actually make it into the seminar materials, adding not only depth but also reality to the teaching points.

I'm forever grateful to those who have shared with me over the years their fears, apprehensions, mistakes, and triumphs in media appearances.

And, being on "the next flight out" basis to take over the media in a crisis event for several large corporations has given me an appreciation for how vulnerable people are when a crisis occurs, especially if they are not prepared.

If this book helps you see communications in a different way, I'm pleased. If it helps you communicate with the media more effectively, I'm very happy. And, if it helps you communicate better with your family and those you love - I'm absolutely ecstatic! For that's my intention.

And, to all of you who have been in my seminars, given so freely of your time, who have come up at breaks and shared personal stories, or have written to me months after a seminar letting me know that something I said had actually changed your life, I thank you from the bottom of my heart!

I know now God wanted me to teach, but I had lots of trials to go through to get there. Don't we all?

"I don't think anyone should write their autobiography until after they're dead."

Samuel Goldwyn
(1882 − 1974)

INDEX

The Heart in Communicating

CHAPTER 1

"Where else could the Elk be?"

As someone once said, "There is no such thing as teaching - only learning. Information must be pulled into the brain willingly, not shoved in."

Whenever I think about that phrase I'm reminded about an early mentor of mine who is long deceased now. We've all had mentors, and the very special ones are few and far between.

In a lifetime, you can probably name only one or two people who have had a profound influence on your life. People who you could go to today and tell them anything and they would give you the honest answer you are searching for and do it with compassion. They are the jewels in our lives and we can only hope to be a true mentor to just one person ourselves.

"Old Chris" the cowboy was just such a mentor to me, and didn't even know it. In my early teens during the summertime, after school let out, I'd work on a huge ranch in southwestern Montana.

They were all huge in Montana - tens of thousands of acres. Haying, chopping wood for the cook-house, milking two cows each morning and running the milk through a separator, building corrals with lodge pole pines we'd cut down by hand and hauled to the home ranch to build corrals or mend the fences with, and of course, branding calves.

One of my favorite things to do was to ride to the "up country" - the federal reserve land, where ranchers would trail their cattle to fatten them up on the upper range grasses while the natural hayfields grew in the valleys down near the home places.

We would cut and stack the hay around August and then bring the cattle back down to the home ranches in the fall before the weather got cold.

Several times during the summer we would head up to the federal reserve range to check the cattle and it was a long ride on horseback. The elevation would go up to 8,500 feet and the scenery was breathtaking.

I can still muster up the incomparably clean smell of riding through sagebrush right after a summer rain. Nothing is quite as intoxicating. They should bottle that!

"Old Chris" was a true cowboy. He probably didn't have a high school education, but he was one of the smartest men I ever met. Country smart. And, he didn't like to talk much. He'd just point out several things and then just sit back and let you figure it out.

He reminded me of the character "Curly" played by Jack Palance in the movie "City Slickers". A tough old cowboy on the outside, Chris had a heart of gold on the inside - if you could manage to get past the gruff exterior.

One day we were riding in the up country checking cattle, and going across a huge meadow. He grabbed a hand-full of reins and stopped, and without saying a word got off his horse and indicated that I should do the same. I did, because I did everything Chris told me to do at that age, sometimes half afraid not to.

There was a thick grove of Aspen trees in the middle of that meadow. We left the horses in the meadow and walked toward the grove of trees. When we got near, Chris put a finger to his lips and we quietly entered the aspens. Inside this large circle of aspens was a much smaller grassy area with a narrow mountain stream running through the middle of it.

Lying down on the bank of the stream was a beautiful cow elk and her tiny calf. It looked like a western oil painting with the sky, the shimmering aspens, the meadow grass, the stream and the elk.

We just stood there taking this all in, and then Chris jerked his thumb backwards signaling it was time to leave. We walked back to the horses who were also enjoying the high mountain grasses.

As we mounted up and continued our ride to check cattle, Chris said nothing. I, on the other hand, had a burning question, but knowing how much Chris hated talking waited as long as I could. About an hour later I couldn't stand it any longer. "Chris", I said, "How'd you know the elk would be there?" As soon as I uttered those words I knew I'd failed to get the message.

Chris stopped his horse, leaned on the saddle horn, tipped his hat back, screwed up his face and looked at me like I was some alien from another planet, and said something like, "Guess I'm going to have to put this into words for you, huh, city slicker?"

He thought the town I grew up in, Dillon, was a city. Well, we did have 3,500 people in the 50's and it's still about the same today. Dillon was hardly a city. We had one stop light for a while, but nobody was coming so they took it out.

But, to Chris, I was that city slicker, and totally unable to see the obvious. To him, I was too pre-occupied with who I was going to be, what I was going to do in life to be an objective observer of the very life that was going on around me. Chris usually let you figure these 'revelations' out your-self, but he knew he was going to have to help me with the "elk discovery theory".

"What time of day was it?"

"About noon", I answered.

"Now, where do you think a mother elk would be with her calf around noon? Somewhere safe? Somewhere hidden maybe, where her calf would be safe and there would be water and feed for her?"

"Yes", I replied.

"Now", he said, further tormenting me with my apparent ignorance, "Which way was the wind blowing? Were we downwind?"

"Yep", I replied.

"So, she couldn't smell us, right?"

"Yep", I said, still not getting it.

"Look at your horse's ears", he said. "The deer flies are biting and he's flapping those things so hard he probably couldn't hear you from where you're sitting in the saddle. Well, the same things happening to the elk's ears. And, we probably could have driven a tractor in there and she wouldn't have heard us.......*Now where else would the elk be!?*"

I got it. He knew instinctively where the elk would be at that time of day. He was tuned into his world and the basic - but real - things around him and just knew they would be there. It was so simple! He truly listened to life around him. He just saw things, as they really were, not obscured by a lot of outside clutter. He didn't over-think anything. He just listened to his heart.

I often think of that story when I see people going about their daily lives, and more profoundly during a crisis event. We fail to communicate our true feelings because we are unable to see the simple, but clear picture with all the professional and personal clutter out there. Those things tend to cloud our own natural radars.

We don't listen with just our ears. A good friend of mine, Phil Clark, a Master Instructor at the National Weather Service Training Center in Kansas City, tells his management and leadership students; "Listening is a full contact sport."

When someone from the media is interviewing you, listen with your face. Be interested as well as interesting to the viewer. Do this in your personal and professional life also. Who would you rather talk to - someone whose face tells you they can't wait for you to stop talking so they can talk, or the person who is actively listening and reacting with their face?

We call that "face time" in television and often the audience makes up its mind whether or not they like you even before you open your mouth just by looking at your face. How many times have you watched a program like "60-Minutes", and seeing someone's face as they are being introduced, come to the immediate conclusion: Guilty!

For almost any disaster or crisis event, your involvement, or your part of the event has a very simple explanation. Quit over-thinking it, as old Chris would say. When you get to the point where you are simply saying it, rather than over-thinking it - you've arrived.

We sift and filter our communications through a variety of screens. Some we learned from childhood, some job related and others from our desire to be an observer to an event, not a participant in it.

One of the keys to crisis communications is to be able to very clearly answer a question and bridge to two things you want your audience to remember or act upon, and then stop.

I often say to a seminar group, "What if I opened that door and told you that you had 8 seconds to tell this city what you would like them to remember about what you do - what would you say?"

Someone will volunteer and usually go into a long explanation, which often resembles the 'history of the world', all with excellent grammar, sentence structure and oral punctuation's. As if it had been written for the eye, not the ear.

I'll say, "What did you mean by that?" They'll counter with a shorter version, and I'll say again, "But, what do you mean?" They'll shorten it again, and I'll say, "I still don't get it - what do you really mean?" Then, as if a light bulb had been turned on, they simply blurt out the obvious and smile as if they've discovered a hidden truth.

In truth, they have. It's so easy once you've re-discovered the secret of communicating from the heart.

Just say what you mean. And, like old Chris, look for the obvious.

The answer is almost always right there.

CHAPTER 2

"The Ionospheric Skip

*E*ven today in this new millennium, many kids are still fascinated by the 50's. Those of us who came of age in that magic decade, and for whom the movie, "American Graffiti" is a personal anthology, have managed to hold on those grounded values and a wonderment of things around us that were instilled in us during that era.

We didn't have television. Well, those of us in Montana didn't until the mid-50's, and then it was black and white and only one channel, which came from Butte.

But, we could still hear the great voices on radio. We played outside, roamed the nearby hills summer and winter, usually with our faithful hunting dogs. We imagined and dreamed.

We weren't cluttered with information coming from all of the sources available to kids today; television, pagers, cell phones, laptops and 24/7 news on dozens of cable channels. Life was simple, and perhaps because of that, we were able to put a lot of life's lessons in perspective.

One of the earliest goals I remember in my teens was to be on the radio. When a local man in our small town of Dillon, Montana, decided to build a radio station on the outskirts of town in 1956, I was thrilled. I was a sophomore in high school, and harbored this strong desire to be one of the first announcers on that station.

I kept walking or hitching a ride after school out to the station, that was about a mile or so North of Dillon in a pasture. It was a small unassuming one-story structure with a big picture window that looked into the broadcast studio, and behind it stood the 200-foot tower. At 15, it might as well have been Radio City and here it was almost in my back yard!

I knew the announcers. They were locals. Well, one was from Butte, about 65 miles to the North, and he was going to Western Montana College in Dillon. But, I thought the three of them were probably the luckiest threesome around.

It was a daylight-to-dark station, at 800 on the AM dial, and I hung out there picking up as much as I could about the radio business.

I ripped the 5 minute summaries off of the AP teletype, edited and organized them, selected the records and stacked them in play order for the disk jockey's, took the transmitter readings for the FCC, and anything else that needed to be done.

I can still remember hearing 3 bells ringing from the AP teletype signifying a bulletin from the Associated Press was about to come in. That was our "breaking news", and unlike today, it usually was breaking news.

High school became a place to study English, debate, public speaking and anything that had to do with getting into radio.

And, adding to this was the fact that my Dad's cousin, Hugh Brundage, was a very famous broadcaster in Hollywood, California.

Hugh had been a staff business writer for the Los Angeles Times in the late 40's when radio was king.

One day, the man who usually did the morning business break on KMPC from the Los Angeles Times over the phone, was sick and Hugh filled in. After the broadcast, the station manager, who happened to be listening at that early hour, called the Times and asked, "Who was that voice this morning?" The station hired Hugh that week.

KMPC was and still is a 50,000 watt clear channel radio station at the corner of Sunset and Vine in Hollywood. Owned then by the movie cowboy legend Gene Autry, it remains today a giant in the industry.

Hugh became KMPC's News Director. He pioneered "Sigalert", a system by which people on the freeways could be notified of traffic delays, which is still in use today. He was the first newsman aboard the first nuclear submarine, "Nautilus".

He later became the first television news anchor on KTLA-TV in Los Angeles, and was also the announcer for the Bob Hope Show for many years.

There was George Fenniman with Groucho Marx, Don Wilson with Jack Benny, and Hugh Brundage with Bob Hope. Needless to say, Hugh Brundage loomed large in my life.

Dillon, Montana, sits just a mile high, with the 'bench' as we called it surrounding it at about 6,000 feet and then the Rocky Mountains, which rose above 10,000 feet. On clear winter nights, I could take my "pre-owned" – we used to say "used" - 1953 Studebaker Coupe up on a gravel road on the bench, park, and tune the AM radio to KMPC, 710 on the dial in Hollywood, and hear that great station.

I could also listen to other great stations like WLS Chicago, and KOMA in Oklahoma. All of this happened with a great deal of clarity on something called the "ionospheric skip". At the right time of year, usually cold, clear winter nights, the AM signals of strong stations bounce off of the ionosphere and return to earth hundreds of miles away from their intended FCC local patterns.

Not only could I hear the great voices, but also the great formats, in news, music and sports. KOMA in Oklahoma was a Todd Storz station, and Todd was the father of "Top 40" radio. It is a format that is still copied today, and I certainly wanted to learn it. I sat there in my "Studie" and wrote down formats and ideas that I would eventually use.

Ironically, some 50 years later I would be asked to be the Master of Ceremonies for the 50th anniversary of "Top 40 Radio" at a formal dinner celebration held in Kansas City. The invitation came from my good friend, Richard Fatherly, who was an icon in the days of Top-40 radio, and today is the voice heard on many national radio and television commercials. I still covet his "pipes".

In attendance were some of the great radio personalities of that time, radio personalities I had listened to through the ionospheric skip in the 50's, but had never met, including Senator Bill Armstrong, from Colorado, who was the first teenage Top 40 disk jockey in the country. I had to pinch myself that night sitting at the head table next to these legends in broadcasting.

Play-by-play sports broadcasting was also fascinating, and I was bound and determined that I would be the play-by-play announcer for the local Dillon station.

Announcers there did everything, from reading advertising copy, the news, weather and sports, as well as being disk jockeys, but no one was doing play-by-play sports.

When I was a junior in high school, I would take a reel-to-reel tape recorder on road trips with the high school basketball team and sit on the bench with the coach and players, and with a hand held microphone, record the game.

At night, in the hotel room, I would play it back and critique myself, gradually getting better each time at painting a picture for my imaginary audience about the game, being both the "play by play announcer" as well as the "color commentator".

Gradually the team players would show up in my hotel room and ask to listen to the game they just finished playing. Then one evening, the coach knocked on my hotel room door and asked to listen to my "broadcast". When he started using my tapes to critique the team, I knew I was about ready.

Later that same year, 1957, our team went to the State Championship, and there I was, the only play-by-play announcer in town, and the only one who really knew all the team players. I was in high school with them. The station hired me to do the play by play for the state tournament and sent one of their announcers to do the color commentary and station breaks.

We won the State Championship in an exciting game that went into double overtime. My voice was almost gone at the end of the game, but I was on the air as a junior in high school at 16 years of age doing play-by-play sports.

I was still hanging out at the station as much as possible, and when an opening came up, one of the other announcers told the owner, "Why don't you hire Brundage? He's here all the time and knows how to run everything." I was hired the next day, and began broadcasting at the princely sum of $1.35 an hour, in 1956.

I was passionately committed to radio and learning all I could about it, wanting nothing more than to be the very best at it. Looking back on this I've seen a remarkable similarity in what young people select for their summer jobs while in high school and what they eventually wind up doing for careers later on.

I often wonder if parents shouldn't take a more active role in helping their children find summer jobs that reflect not only their personality but also their passions and talents. I can't help think that we might develop a generation of real creative "doers" who would passionately pursue a career and actually make a difference in their chosen fields. Speaking of generational dilemmas, I was about to encounter mine.

If there is a teaching point to all of this, perhaps it's just this: If you're passionately committed to what you're doing, it's contagious.

When you respond to the media during any event, crisis or not, your body language as well as the *way* you express yourself will tell your audience much more about you than the words you speak.

People don't care how much you know until they know how much you care.

CHAPTER 3

"The 4th Generation Dilemma"

*N*ow here's where this journey takes a little twist. It was also the beginning of why I'm able to relate to the physiological responses we all exhibit, especially during a crisis event.

This period in my life provided the educational background and perspective to the reporting I did later on in life. Especially when I produced and anchored a nationally syndicated series of news programs entitled, "Healthcare Business Review".

My father was a third generation funeral director in Dillon, as was his father and his grandfather - my great grandfather. However, it was my great grandfathers brother, Everett Hiram Brundage, who brought the first printing presses to Virginia City, Montana during the gold rush, and later to Dillon.

So there it was - a huge fork in the Brundage tree. One Brundage was a funeral director and the other a journalist. I would wrestle initially from this strange dichotomy, but it would help me later when teaching my seminars.

Needless to say, my father wanted the fourth generation in the funeral home, and I apparently was it. My older brother, Lew, had joined the Navy, and my younger sister, Carol, was still in grade school. My mother was trained as an RN, a surgical nurse, and was an absolute treasure. She always helped my father in the business and wanted me there also.

Mortuary college at that time was an intensive 3 semesters, followed by 2 years of internship, more college and national as well as state board examinations. The state board exams, as I recall, were 8 hours a day for two days.

I was sent to the California College of Mortuary Science in Los Angeles. (Later I would come back to Dillon, go to the University of Montana Western, and study for a degree in Biological Science.) Now, I could have been sent to St. Louis, Chicago or New York to Mortuary College, but in a fortunate twist of fate for me, and a tactically bad decision for my father, he decided I should attend his alma mater and I went to L.A.

Entering my life again, my father's cousin, Hugh Brundage, the now very famous radio and television broadcaster and announcer for the Bob Hope Show. He had the number one newscast in the entire city of Los Angeles, and billboards with his picture and the KMPC logo on the busses and freeways proclaimed this. He was also the television news anchor on KTLA, the first commercial television station to broadcast west of the Mississippi River.

I remember spending as much time as possible during those intensive semesters in college there with Hugh at the radio station. I had no car in Los Angeles, so I would catch the bus which stopped near the college and make the several transfers necessary to arrive at Sunset and Vine in Hollywood. I got to know that bus route fairly well.

Hugh knew something that my father probably did also, but didn't acknowledge, or didn't want to acknowledge until in his later years. That I was not only 'interested' in radio, I'd already had several years experience in it and was pretty good at it.

I don't know if I was actively pursuing some sort of subliminal career at that time or whether it was just that early awareness that people sometimes have when they know they have a natural inclination for something.

My father was a great man, and like so many fathers, he often saw my future through his eyes. He graduated Suma Cum Laude from the California College of Mortuary Science, was the President of the Montana Funeral Directors Association, and a Board Member of the National Funeral Directors Association. He obviously wanted the next generation to follow in his footsteps.

As a personal side note, I remember much later on when my father was in his 60's and came to visit us in Kansas City. By then, I owned a video production company, was still directing some news programs and also ran the network's cameras in the Kansas City Royals dugout during the American League games. (I talk more about that in Chapter 17).

During one of his visits, I had an afternoon game scheduled for NBC, and asked the network director if I could get a network crew badge and pass for my visiting father. I did, and he accompanied me that day. What an experience. I got to watch my father in my world.

At the stadium, we went in the Kansas City Royals entrance, through a phalanx of people waiting for player's autographs. We were greeted at the clubhouse door by security and had our badges checked. I'm pretty sure my father loved the idea of being on a network sports staff for the day.

We got on the Royals elevator and went down and exited in their locker room. We walked down the tunnel the players take to the dugout which was where my camera position was located.

Now my father was very capable of hiding his emotions, but very astute at taking everything in around him. He didn't say too much. I think he was just enjoying the sensory overload that was surrounding him at that time.

Growing up in Montana in the 20's, he was a baseball fan, as were most of the kids in that time period when baseball was "America's pastime", and listened on the radio to the games with his brothers. I'm pretty sure he'd never been to a major league baseball game in person, so emerging from the tunnel onto the playing field with the crowd noise, surrounded by players warming up for the game was pretty exciting.

I found a seat for him right in the dugout and he sat with players like George Brett, Frank White and Bo Jackson. I introduced him around, and after the game took him into the NBC production truck and showed him how a game was produced and aired. He was very interested in everything, again just taking it in.

I never knew how much of an impression that day had on him until several years later when I was visiting Dillon. His life long friend, an attorney by the name of Leonard Schultz, pulled me aside one day.

He and my father were not only friends, they had golfed together for years, had lost their wives to illness while in their 60's, and generally depended on each other for that support we'll all need later in life.

One evening, when we were all at Leonard's house for cocktails prior to going to dinner, he told me how proud my father was of me, and what a tremendous success I'd made out of my life. My father apparently had come back to Dillon and told his best friend what he couldn't tell me. That for years he had wished I'd have been the "4th generation in the Brundage Funeral Home, but he knew now that was wrong. I was a much better in television because that's where my passion was.

After watching me direct television programs, be part of a network television crew at a major league baseball game and run my own video production company, he became convinced that I was doing what I was cut out to do and doing it pretty well.

But, it was through Dad's best friend that I really learned that I was not only alright, but had achieved a pinnacle of success far greater than what I probably would have risen to had I stayed in the family business.

It seemed that I often found out how I was doing through my father's friends. He was in many ways an "old Montana cowboy". He'd brag on me to his friends, but never to me. I suspect a lot of fathers do the same, never realizing that most sons simply want their father's affirmation.

Most sons see their fathers as someone they would like to aspire to, many times not following in their foot-steps, but carving out new territory for a career, but always seeking their fathers' approval.

I guess that is why, in a large part, I agreed to go to Los Angeles to college, to get that approval rating.

But, I also knew Hugh Brundage was on the air there at KMPC and had listened to him on that "Ionospheric skip" growing up in Montana.

CHAPTER 4

"Give me a sense of"

*O*ne of the most important lessons I learned from Hugh Brundage in those early years was the absolute necessity for clear writing and even clearer on-air delivery.

Whenever I could get away from a class at college, I would hop a bus and get to KMPC's studios in Hollywood. I'd find Hugh either in the newsroom or the large radio news studio with its microphone hanging down over the anchor desk.

I'd watch and listen as he did the morning 5-minute news reports every half hour. When he would finish and punch the "off air" button, he would often hand me the script and say, "Rewrite the lead". I did, and then he'd say, "Read it to me". I would, and sometimes he would say, "No no. What's the most important word in that sentence? Your listeners can't go back and 're-hear' you; they have to get it the first time, objectively and with clarity so that they can make up their own minds."

His remarks have stayed with me over the years. And, in my seminars today, I always tell my students the same thing. When you write or deliver a 'sound bite', your viewers and listeners have to get it the *first* time, with no spin on your voice - objectively - and with such clarity that they can then make decisions of their own about the story and what it means to them. Equally important, based on the way you *say* things, they make decisions about you as a person.

Too often today, the media tries to make 'closure' for us, and in doing so, creates an often distorted or shallow view of the story, making it virtually impossible to come to any conclusion other than the one they are advancing.

There seems to be very few real investigative reports anymore, and certainly very little reporting on the issues that truly affect us all. Television had managed to make almost every issue a sensational sound bite, and the more tantalizing, scandalous or unsavory the better.

"If it bleeds it leads."

Admittedly it's difficult to point a camera at a school bond issue. It's much easier to point it at a burning overturned tanker truck. But is that "news"? One of the first questions I ask my seminar participants is to give me a one sentence definition of news. I ask them, "If I were in 5th grade, and you were my teacher, how would you define "news"?

It's difficult isn't it? I get all kinds of answers, like "It's history in the making". "It's what happened today". "Something of interest to me".

"Facts about a series of events." (I wish that were the case.)

Let me give you a definition of "news" you won't find in any journalism textbook. It's something I came up with in my mental meanderings that night in Anchorage, Alaska, trying to put some academic handles on things I knew instinctively so that I could teach my first media response seminar the next morning.

My definition of news is simply this: *"News are those events that happen outside the parameters of normal behavior."*

It could be very good news, or very bad news. Most of what we do everyday is not news. That's why we tend to get so worked up when the media comes calling. Everything goes right for weeks, and then some tragedy happens and there they are with cameras and microphones.

In the old days, we knew what news was, or at least when Walter Cronkite said, "That's the way it is", we pretty much had a sense that that's the way it was. What made Walter so credible? Was it his delivery? His "grandfatherly" appearance? Or, maybe it was the fact that for the most part he simply gave us the facts, and gave us the common courtesy of making up our own minds.

I do recall that when he came back from Vietnam and aired his one-hour documentary on Vietnam, President Lyndon Johnson decided not to run again. He was quoted as saying, "If I've lost Cronkite, I've lost the war."

But, today with hundreds of cable channels, 24-hour news programs springing up around the country, there is such a rush to be first that facts sometimes take a second seat.

They call it "news gathering" today, not "news reporting", and therein lies some of the problem. It's not just semantics. When you are 'gathering' the news, you don't have the facts – the complete picture, so the media often speculates. When more complete facts come in they can change their casualty figures, damage reports or other facts they didn't originally have.

This is a drastic departure from the way we used to report news. We had to have at least 2 confirmations on major stories to air them.

Who could forget after President Reagan and Presidential News Secretary James Brady were shot, how the media in their rush to be first, reported on the incident?

NBC and CBS went on the air and reported that the President was shot and taken to the hospital, and James Brady was also shot and was dead. Brady, of course, was not dead, but no one watching those two networks knew that.

Frank Reynolds, ABC's veteran anchor went on the air with the story, and during the broadcast you could see him being handed a piece of paper - off stage. He paused, looked at the paper and turned to the person off stage who had handed it to him and exclaimed, "Dammit, I'm not reading that on the air – get me two confirmations!"

What he had been handed was the same report that the other networks were broadcasting, that James Brady was dead. To ABC's credit they didn't air that.

The rush for ratings is becoming so intense that facts are beginning to take a back seat to being first. So many news channels are springing up, cable channels and internet news services, "blogs", that the old networks are becoming concerned about "shares" and how they are going to pay their talent and keep the high revenues from advertisers.

Right after 9-11, I picked up on a new phrase for speculation. On that terrible day September 11th, 2001, anchors became anchors again. There was so much information – so many "facts" coming in from the field in Pennsylvania, the Pentagon and from New York, - that all anchors could do was gather the facts and give them to the public. Once again they were actually reporting "news".

But, as the facts diminished, the need to fill the 24/7 airtimes did not. Often you would hear an anchor utter the phrase, "give us a sense of" to some correspondent out in the field who would then have to speculate on what was about to happen. Why they don't just say - "guess"!

The worst cases are when you see reporters, interviewing other reporters about something they 'heard' from other reporters!

Good reporting requires the reporter to give the story its perspective. Why is this story important to the viewer? What impact can or will it have? Historically what has been the significance of this kind of event or action?

Since the media has in many cases abdicated this responsibility, it is incumbent on those who must respond - through the media - to a target audience to give the story its true perspective; the rest of the story.

It's your job when interviewed by the media to provide that perspective to the audience. And, there are very tried and true methods for doing just that, as we'll discover later on.

CHAPTER 5

"Minor Gods and Four Stars"

*W*hen I returned to Dillon, from Los Angeles, life was never quite the same. I practiced with Dad in the family funeral business, but also was asked to do some radio programming there which I did whenever possible. I also was enrolled at the University of Montana-Western in Dillon, studying for my degree in Biological Science.

It was there that I met my wife, Gail. I was 21, senior class president, and she was a 19 year-old sophomore cheerleader majoring in elementary education. All our friends thought it was the perfect match. We got married in 1962, in Dillon, at Saint James Episcopal Church. We spent the next 3 years in Dillon. I worked with Dad in the family business and Gail and I had our first child, Kelly. She was blond and beautiful – an absolute delight, and life seemed about as good as it could get.

It was the mid-60's by then, and the draft was still very much alive, Vietnam was escalating, and knowing my days were numbered, I joined the

Army and went to OCS (Officer Candidate School).

I graduated number one in my class and was commissioned a 2nd Lieutenant in Armor. My first assignment was as a Platoon Leader in Company B, 3rd Battalion, 77th Armor, at Fort Carson, Colorado. . Gail, Kelly and I packed up and moved to Colorado.

I wanted to get the Army experience behind me, and knowing that following in Dad's footsteps in the funeral profession as the 5th generation was not what I wanted to do, I knew I could get both public information and television experience in the Army that would serve me well later on.

First assignments always produce indelible memories. As a Platoon Leader, and a brand new 2nd Lieutenant, I got to do about everything in the company, from being mess officer - overseeing the daily feeding and caring of the troops - to the maintenance of our aging tank fleet.

Most of the new tanks were being shipped to Vietnam, and we still had a mixture of both type of tanks. The old gas M-48's and the newer diesel M-60A1's. The old tanks were carryovers from Korean War days and had far less power than the newer diesel ones. The new ones had 1,200 hp, turbo-charged engines and far superior armament systems as well as speed and maneuverability.

In that memorable year, I trained AIT (Advanced Individual Training – the next step after BCT - Basic Combat Training) troops in

Armor tactics. We trained on the ranges at Fort Carson, and also loaded the tanks on rail cars and took them out to the Desert Training Center at Fort Erwin, California. Death Valley.

Most all of the troops I trained were destined for Vietnam, and I drilled them hard knowing before they did where they were headed.

I was promoted to 1st Lieutenant at Fort Carson, and was given command of Company B. By that time, we had a new group of trainees to put through their 10-week cycle. I was getting used to the long days that a company commander endures, and felt a keen responsibility to the troops in my command.

I was only 24 years old at the time, but even the seasoned NCO's called me "the old man", a term reserved for the commander of a unit. Looking back, I was still pretty green, and learned a lot from those older NCO's. They were the pros and I was the student.

The Army likes to have their officers trained in several different fields. Since I had experience in broadcasting before entering the service, they also entered the specialty, PAO, (Public Affairs Officer) in my official personnel record.

The highest-ranking officer on post was, of course, the Post Commander, a Major General – a two star. I thought he was at least a "minor god". Then, one day we received word that Creighton Abrams, the Army Chief of Staff would be visiting. He wanted to visit a tank platoon and ride a tank, and then address a group of us who also served as Public Affairs Officers.

I remember the day he arrived. I don't know if any of the other officers did this, but I counted his stars. He had twenty stars on! Four on each of his field jacket epaulets, four on each of his shirt collars, and four across his helmet. He had to qualify as a "major god".

He rode my tank, and thankfully it worked. I have no idea what I would have said or done had it not worked, as it was prone to do so often during normal training exercises.

After that minor success in the field, General Abrams assembled a group of officers who were PAO's, and proceeded to tell us about media relations. I thought, "What does this guy know about public information?" He was a combat veteran, who, as a Lieutenant Colonel under Patton in WWII, spearheaded an Armor Battalion across Europe. A great tanker.

(Incidentally, 5 years later when I was on my second Vietnam tour, I was selected as the Commander of Troops for the change of command over there, and General Abrams, Lieutenant General Southerland, Lieutenant General Zais and I passed in review before all the flags of the nations involved in the Vietnam War. He sent me an autographed picture taken by an AP photographer, with the inscription, "To Captain Brundage – Thanks for a job well done on June 17th, 1970") It hangs in my office to this day.

But, one thing he said that day has stayed with me ever since. Even when doing broadcast news later on, and certainly when teaching my seminars.

He told us one reason the media didn't trust us was that they thought we only went to them when we had a good story. And, the reason we don't trust the media is that we don't think they're going to tell the story the way we would like it told. True enough, I thought.

He then went on to say, "If you're the PAO at Fort Carson, you're going to have 10 stories a year that will hit the media. Five will be good, and five will be bad. If you release the same amount of information on the bad story as you do on the good story each time, watch what happens to your credibility with the press at the end of the year. It will go sky high."

How did a crusty, cigar chewing Army Chief of Staff arrive at that succinct conclusion? Through trail and error I'm guessing, and certainly through observations made throughout his career. And, how right he was then, and still is today.

If you have a news story that's about to break, it doesn't make any difference if it's bad or good – call the media first. Don't make them call you. If you want to control a crisis or negative situation, take control from the beginning. Don't try to wrest control later on. It doesn't work that way.

If you go to the media with a bad news story before it breaks, they are much more apt to listen to your side and give you the benefit of the doubt than if they have to call you and try to get details after the fact.

I was only to be there at Fort Carson a year before getting my first orders to Vietnam. Gail was 8 months pregnant with our second child at the time I received my orders, and we moved back to Dillon, so that Gail could be close to both her family and mine during my year in Vietnam.

I had 30 days leave, and in January, just 10 days prior to my departure, our son was born. Kerry came into the world at Barrett Hospital in Dillon, and he was perfect in every way. I wanted to do anything rather than go to Vietnam in 10 days! I couldn't believe I had a new son whose first year I would never know.

My tour in Vietnam was to last one year, and it was, up to that point, the most difficult separation I had ever experienced. Those of you who have experienced long separations from loved ones during combat understand exactly what I went through at that time.

Dad and Mom spent a lot of time with both Kelly and Kerry during that year, getting to know their grandchildren

CHAPTER 6

"First Tour RVN"

*A*fter my initial active duty assignment at Fort Carson, Colorado, I went to the Republic of Vietnam, in 1967, as a First Lieutenant, and was assigned to a cavalry unit in the 199th Light Infantry Brigade, in III Corps, south of Saigon.

I'll never forget that first night in the "repo-depot", the replacement center in Long Bien. No one knew anyone. We were all "long-timers" newly arrived in Vietnam and awaiting orders to some yet unknown unit. The "short-timers", those about to leave to return to the U.S., were partying in a beer tent not far away.

I laid awake that night, all night, listening to the unfamiliar sounds of war. In the distance I could hear helicopters, and what sounded like artillery batteries responding to a fire mission. An occasional loud 'crump' meant someone was getting some 'incoming' and not too far away. It was one of the longest and loneliest nights of my life.

I got my assignment the next morning from the posting outside the personnel tent. There was another Lieutenant who came to pick me up in a jeep. He said that I was replacing a Lieutenant who had just gotten shot on night ambush. That wasn't exactly what I needed to hear on an empty stomach half way around the world.

We drove west and then south of Saigon, now Ho Chi Minh City, until we arrived at a place called Cat Lai, which was the forward headquarters for the 199th Infantry Brigade, light/separate. The combat brigade had three infantry battalions, an artillery battery, and one armored cavalry troop. I was assigned to D-Troop, 17th Armored Cavalry.

When I got to the unit area, I found there were no armored personnel carriers, no tanks or the other vehicles and equipment I had learned about and trained on, that were associated with an armored cavalry unit.

The Company Commander, Captain Mike Small, from Boston, was a well-educated and reserved commander, and one I thought perfect for the position. He informed me that this troop had been assigned boats instead!

Our mission was to set up and conduct 'riverine operations' or night ambushes on jungle rivers in our AO (area of operations). And, to document those tactics for use in classes at the Armor School at Fort Knox, since apparently we were the first armored cavalry unit to do this. We also had the first "starlight scopes" in the Army, which attached to our rifles and amplified the night sky allowing us to see the enemy much better than he could see us.

As the senior 1st Lieutenant, I was made Executive Officer of D Troop. The "XO" wore a lot of hats including making sure that the troop had all its equipment up and running, personnel slots were filled, as well as filling in for the Troop Commander when he was called away. I frequently filled in as Troop Commander.

I would also overfly areas where Brigade intelligence suspected the VC were infiltrating at night, using these jungle rivers to transport both men and equipment. I would do this in a light observation helicopter (LOH or "loach" as we called them.) The loach had no firepower, so we would fly low and fast over the jungle areas, the pilot executing some tight turns as I would follow the map and direct him to the suspect areas.

My job was not only to observe any activity in those areas, but also to locate and pinpoint on the map where the Troop could effectively take the boats and set up a night ambush position that evening. I also marked secondary ambush sites in case, for whatever reason, the primary site would be compromised.

I would then go back and brief the platoon leader of the platoon that would be going out that night. We rotated the three platoons through night ambush duty. One night on and two off. Showing the platoon leader and the platoon sergeant both the primary and secondary ambush sites on the map of the AO, I would also show them the best river routes in and out of the area.

We would often travel some 10 miles on these rivers with twists and turns and small tributaries that had to be mapped and memorized. Getting lost at night on a jungle river was not an option I even wanted to think about. I did have nightmares about that years later.

To avoid compromising our position for that night's ambush site, the only people who would know the ambush site location besides me were the CO, Brigade intelligence and Brigade artillery, in case we needed artillery fire support during the night.

Then, I would go to the boat landing and make sure that the maintenance was being done on the motors and the boats.

When I took over as XO, they were using 35 hp Johnson outboards. Hardly enough engine power to move the steel Boston Whalers, let alone 8 men armed to the teeth. They were sitting ducks out there on the river moving at 5 miles an hour!

Not long after arriving, and observing this situation, I told my driver, John Housenetch, who everyone called "groundhog", to saddle up. We were going into Saigon to see the Commanding General of 1st Logistics' Command. He was the general who was ultimately responsible for all equipment in Vietnam.

On the way into Saigon, my first trip since arriving in Vietnam, I noticed a small lake near the outskirts where some soldiers in swimming suits were water skiing! Their two boats had huge 125 hp Evinrudes! That made my case.

We had combat troops going out on the river at night with 35 hp outboards, and these "khaki swine" as we called the support personnel in the rear areas, were water skiing behind 125 hp outboards!

I assure you my driver and I weren't in khaki's. We were in jungle fatigues, helmets, AR-15's Colt Commando's, grenades taped to our field gear and generally pretty grungy looking.

We pulled up in front of 1st Log Command, and I told Groundhog to wait in the jeep. I went directly to the Commanding General's office, where an aide promptly stopped me and asked if he could help.

Now, I knew the young Captain wasn't going to help, he just didn't want me to go barging into the generals office. So I said it just loud enough so that the General on the other side of the door had to hear; "No, Captain, you can't. I just saw men water-skiing behind powerful outboard motors my men need just to stay alive at night on the jungle rivers south of here. So, unless you can sign some of those over to me, I need to talk to the General."

It worked. Before the Captain could answer, the general opened his door and told me to come in. He gave me the quick up and down, and must have been convinced by the amount of dirt on me that I wasn't located anywhere near Saigon where they go out for lunch everyday and have their 'hooch maids" spit shine their boots daily.

He sat down behind his desk and said something about being pretty gutsy to just walk in and demand equipment. But, then hastened to ask, what unit, how many men per boat, how many boats, etc. He was pretty interested in our unique mission. He then asked, "How many outboards do you want?" I told him we had four boats, and I would like two outboards for each. One running, and the other in maintenance. A total of eight.

He said, "Do you have a truck."

I replied, "No sir, but I can get one here."

He said, "No, we'll deliver. Give my aide exact directions on how to get there and we'll have them there in the morning."

I thanked him, saluted and left. I told Groundhog to get out of here before they change their minds.

Sure enough, the next morning a "deuce and a half" (a 2½ ton cargo truck) pulled into our troop area and unloaded one of the most beautiful sights I'd ever seen. Eight brand new 125 hp outboards.

I hadn't had time to tell the Troop Commander, Captain Small, what I'd done, but he approached the truck and with a smile on his face pulled me aside.

I tried to explain what I did, but he said he already heard from the Brigade Commander, a Colonel, who got a call from the Commanding General at 1st Log Command in Saigon; something about a 1st Lieutenant from D Troop who came storming into his office with a "verbal requisition". While the candor was appreciated, he, the CG of 1st Log would appreciate it if proper channels were followed the next time an equipment issue comes up.

I can only remember Captain Small grinning through the whole reprimand and telling me not to do that again.

Almost every night I would be one of the boat drivers taking the platoon up river to the night ambush position. Sometimes I would stay, but most of the time I would unload the troops and then bring the boats back to the docks at Cat Lai, the troop headquarters. Often the other boat driver and I would travel alone on miles of dark jungle rivers.

With the new engines, we could really move along at night, especially if the tide and current were with us. It was a very dangerous time and the two boats were extremely vulnerable to enemy fire on the return trip. The other boat driver and I simply hunkered down and pushed the throttle full forward, trying to remember all the twists and turns on the way back. We had no lights, and if there wasn't a moon out, it was about as black as it could get.

It was a year that took me completely away from broadcasting and or anything remotely associated with it.

But I also learned a lot about who I was. Being responsible for the lives of 18 to 20 year old's in combat is serious business.

Reporting on military activities later in life, I would always remember the heroics of absolutely ordinary people; farm boys from Nebraska, city kids from Chicago. They will always have my undying admiration. They, and the veterans of other foreign wars, made this country what it is.

When I returned stateside, exactly one year later, I was assigned to Fort Knox as a student in the Armor Officer's Advanced Course. Now a Captain, I thought I'd get this one-year course behind me, leave active duty, join the Army Reserves and go back into radio and then television as a civilian. I had a plan. Kelly was 6 and Kerry was 2.

During the year in Armor School, I managed an internship at the Army's only color television studios, which were located on Fort Knox, learning everything from camera operation to directing, writing and producing. I also got a two-week leave from the class to attend the Broadcast Officers School at Fort Benjamin Harrison, Indiana. That gave me another official "military occupational specialty" or MOS - Broadcasting.

CHAPTER 7

"Saigon busy - I give you Bangkok"

*U*nfortunately, on graduation day from the Armor Officer Advanced Course, they announced that Armor Officers, and in fact, most of us in that graduating class were being *sent back* to Vietnam because of the casualty rate among company grade Infantry officers. Most of us in that class had just come back from there less than 12 months ago!

One of the senior officers from the personnel office at Fort Knox got up on the stage before graduation and read off each of our names, and there were about 150 officers in my class. Each name was called and their assignment was read out loud. "Brady, Germany, Branden, Fort Hood, Brundage, Vietnam".

You cannot imagine my utter disappointment or the emptiness that I felt that day. My orders were to take over a tank company in Pleiku, up in the highlands of Vietnam. My plans for leaving active duty, getting in the Army Reserves and going back into broadcasting had just been dashed, and there was a very good chance that I wouldn't escape being wounded or worse from a second tour in Vietnam! The utter emptiness I felt in having to leave my family again – for another year was unimaginable. I distinctly remembered how long that first year was, and I was about to repeat it.

I had been extremely lucky on three very distinct occasions during my first tour. Those memories are indelible as they are for most combat veterans. The Tet Offensive had just begun and the casualties were alarming.

I took all 50 copies of my orders and drove to Louisville, Kentucky, about 20 miles north of Fort Knox, and went to a store that made rubber stamps. I ordered a 2" long stamp and red stamp inkpad. The stamp read "Broadcast Officer".

I promptly stamped all 50 copies of my orders at the top with the red stamp, packed and went back to Vietnam. (In retrospect, I'm sure that act would have resulted in at least a reprimand if discovered, but at the time it seemed like a good idea.)

I took 30 days leave and moved my family back to Dillon so that Gail, Kelly and Kerry could have as much family as possible around them for that year, and Gail could finish her degree at Western Montana College. She graduated in June with a BA in Elementary Education.

I'll never forget my departure – saying goodbye to my family again from the Butte, Montana airport. The jet plane that arrived that day flew through a rainbow on final approach and I took a picture of it. I still have it, and to this day it evokes memories of the absolute beauty and immeasurable sadness of the moment.

When I arrived at Cam Rahn Bay, one of the huge induction and replacement centers in Vietnam, I went immediately to the administrative offices to process my orders. The Specialist who looked at them said, "Ah, Captain Brundage, you're going to take over a tank company in Pleiku".

I responded, "No, look at those orders again, Specialist. See that stamp, 'Broadcast Officer?' Now, get me Armed Forces Network in Saigon on the phone." Those of you reading this who are Vietnam veterans will appreciate the following.

From Cam Rhan Bay to Saigon via telephone line was almost impossible. There were multiple Vietnamese operators to go through who were just as likely to connect you to Thailand as to the number you really wanted, and the lines were always going down.

They had been taught when an officer asked to be connected - you connected him - no matter where! You would hear things like, "Saigon busy - I give you Bangkok".......click, ring. You didn't know anybody in Bangkok, and didn't want to talk to anyone in Bangkok, but all the Saigon circuits were busy and the operator was going to connect you somewhere. She had fulfilled her mission!

By some electronic miracle, I was connected directly to the office of the Commanding Officer, AFNVN, (Armed Forces Network Vietnam) in Saigon! Before I could get cut off through the multiple connections, I quickly informed Colonel Johnson that I had been in broadcasting prior to entering the Army, and was also a graduate Broadcast Officer from DINFOS (the Defense Information School), was on my 2nd tour in Vietnam, and would very much like to get an AFNVN tour on my record.

He seemed genuinely excited to hear from me. The real reason, I suspect, was that there was such a call for combat company grade officers, his replacement needs were on the bottom of the list.

Whatever the reason, he asked if I would take a "temporary assignment" until he could get me to Saigon and AFNVN Headquarters. I, of course, said yes. He said would I consider commanding the Press Center at Phu Bai? I said yes, and where is Phu Bai? He responded that it was the northern-most press camp in country and was located not far from the DMZ (i.e., about 500 miles North of Saigon!)

He assured me that I would be there only a short time and then he would have me reassigned to Saigon and AFNVN. I never did get to Saigon that year, but the Press Center assignment proved to be one of the most valuable experiences of my life, particularly in terms of providing insights and real experience in handling "crisis communications".

I learned what real reporting was like, and what ingredients went into making solid reporters. I also found out what real 'risk communications' was all about, and how to handle a crisis event. I knew whom I could trust with breaking information, and how to break down those barriers that exist between the media and government, the media and the professions, and the media and industry.

Those barriers exist today because of reasons I mentioned before. The media doesn't think we're going to give them the whole story, and we don't think that the media will tell the story the way we want - or at the very least put it into perspective. Both are valid points and demonstrate the need to establish credibility with the media *long* before a crisis event happens.

I tell my clients to go to the media when you have a bad story you know is going to 'go public' just like you would with a good story. And give the same release of information that you would with the good story. Again, give reporters all the information they can get from some other source. Let it come from you.

Just be honest and you'll be credible. In the bridging chart you will see later on, if you don't answer the question honestly, there will be no credibility to the themes that follow.

Today, I won't work for an organization that won't do two absolute essentials during a crisis event. One, tell the truth. Period. And, two, give the reporters all the information they can get from some other source - let it come from you. If you do just those two things, you'll control the crisis. If you don't, the crisis will control you.

That second year in Vietnam at the Press Center, I did what we affectionately called, "The 5-O'clock Follies"- the daily briefings for all the correspondents from around the world. There were hundreds of correspondents from around the world in Vietnam at that time. But, up in Phu Bai, very near the DMZ, we only saw the serious journalists. Some of the others came up, but most left the same day on *any* aircraft going south. There was a war up there.

We were not only close to the action, we flew them in to places where they could get pictures and stories. In some ways, that assignment was more dangerous than running night ambushes on those jungle rivers on my first tour!

During that year, I conducted press briefings on the Mi Lai Massacre, made numerous helicopter trips to the A Shau Valley, Con Tien, Hue, and other totally "hot LZ's" (landing zones) with media who really wanted to get the story first hand.

That second tour in Vietnam also resulted in a divorce. Perhaps it was the times, being separated for parts of 1967-68-69-70, getting married so young, "the 60's", the strain of military life with its constant uncertainties, and a future yet undefined. I do know that many of my fellow Officers experienced the same thing, and I've talked with many in the years following, who were also trying to come to grips with what was happening abroad and here in the U.S. I wouldn't want to repeat that decade for anything, and yet I wouldn't have wanted to miss having Kelly and Kerry in my life for anything either. They were, and are precious.

The Heart in Communicating

CHAPTER 8

"The U.S. Army TV News Team"

*W*hen I returned from that 2nd tour in Vietnam, I was assigned to Fort Knox again. It was Christmas, and most of the Fort was on leave, so I delayed signing in and getting my assignment until I could talk to the Chief of the Television Department at the Armor School - who was also on Christmas leave. (For about 2 weeks there, I think I was unofficially AWOL.)

As soon as the civilian head of the television department came back, I was in his office. He remembered me from my year at the Armor School and my internship at the television studios. I told him that I wanted to work for him and learn everything I could about color television.

He called the Fort Knox Personnel Office and had me personally assigned to him. In six months I was promoted to Chief of Production, responsible for two 18-wheel tractor-trailer vans completely equipped with the latest mobile color television equipment, and state of the art studios on the post. I had died and gone to heaven!

We also produced programs for Army posts around the country for the next two years - more extremely valuable experience. I was in no hurry to exit the active Army now for several reasons. I was getting the finest television production education I could imagine, getting paid to do it, and had control of the finest color television equipment available in the country at that time.

One day, I saw an article in *The Army Times* about a one of a kind unit being formed, called, the "U.S. Army Television News Team". I was on that in a flash! I called for an audition and made arrangements to get out to Kansas City, Missouri, where the U.S. Army News Center was located.

By 1971, I had already completed flight training and had my Private Pilots license and was well on my way to getting my Commerical Pilots license. I rented a plane from Fort Knox and flew myself out to Kansas City that week.

They already had a Captain on orders who was enroute from an overseas assignment, and was scheduled to be there in two weeks. But apparently I passed the audition interview process so well, that when I walked out the door, the Commander of the News Center called the Pentagon and said to cancel the orders on the Captain who was coming, and put me on orders as the new Chief of the U.S. Army Television News Team.

This was truly a gift. The Army Television News Team was a one of a kind organization consisting of just three people. I got to select my cameraman and producer/writer, which I did from contacts I'd made at the Press Center in Vietnam, the Broadcast Officers School in Indianapolis and on Fort Knox - all media experiences.

My first, and only choice for my writer-producer was a SFC (Sergeant First Class) by the name of Matt Glasgow. Matt had served under me in Vietnam at the Press Center in Phu Bai near the DMZ, and then at the DaNang Press Center, a large facility that housed all the major network crews.

Matt was extraordinary. He was a bonifide member of Mensa. Mensa is the international genius organization. I know because he took the exam right there in Vietnam, sent it in and was immediately accepted. Matt was the most brilliant writer I'd ever met.

He would go across the DaNang River early in the morning to XXIV Corps Headquarters and get the intelligence briefing notes and then come back and write the briefing for me to deliver that day at the "5-0'clock Follies".

There were a couple of days, I am pretty sure he didn't go over to the headquarters and just made this stuff up! But, above all, he was the most loyal, competent NCO I'd ever met in the Army.

When I called him in Germany, where he was headquartered with the U.S. Army in Frankfort, I no sooner said, "Hi Matt, this is Captain Brundage". He replied, "When do you want me there, Skipper"? I explained the position of writer-producer for the new concept – the U.S. Army Television News Team.

He interrupted and said again, "When do you want me there, sir? "I don't care what we're doing as long as you're the boss."

"In two weeks if you can make it", I replied. I had been given carte blanche on my selections for that position and the position of cinematographer. Matt, true to his word, was there two weeks later.

Picking the cinematographer was a daunting task for me. We had to have someone who could shoot film in very hostile environments.

He needed to be a consummate professional as the end result had to make "network air" according to our directives. He needed to not only have superior shooting skills, he also had to be the film editor.

Matt said, "I know the person we need, and you know him too." His name was Marty Blackmore, and he was certainly qualified. At the time he was the cinematographer for the Secretary of Defense. I did remember meeting him at least once at the DaNang Press Center when he would come to visit Matt.

I thought I'd be pushing the envelope to try and liberate the "Sec Def's" personal cinematographer, but they had made quite a point out of saying you can have anyone you want in the Army for those two positions.

I requested Marty be assigned, and within 30

days, he was there. We had what I thought then, and know now, was the finest television news team in the business – period.

When we got together as a team, I trained the crew on the latest formats for television news, flew out to Hollywood and bought the latest film cameras that the networks were using, CP-16's.

My mission was simple. The Army wanted me to take the team to places that the civilian media couldn't go, and produce television news stories. Our only caveat was that we had to get them on the air - network air. We couldn't wear uniforms and had to adhere to network formatting.

What a job! And I had the greatest boss in the world; a Lieutenant Colonel by the name of Earl Beatty. He gave me free rein and held me accountable. He was from the old "Patton" school. General Patton would say, "Give someone a mission, expect them to do it, then get the hell out of their way and be amazed at the results!"

LTC Beatty was that kind of man.

(LTC Beatty passed away in 2005, and I went down to his funeral at Fort Sam Houston, Texas. His family and I sat around together after the service doing "remember whens" about a great man at a great time in history for all of us.)

No one could have asked for more. All of us on the team were single, and I had a blank airline ticket book. We could literally go anywhere in the world as long as our stories made network air.

Our apartment managers loved us. We'd be in town long enough to launder clothes, pay the rent and go out again.

We reported on the de-mining of the Suez Canal, were on Cyprus before the riots, did reports from Checkpoint Charlie on the Berlin Wall, and were in war torn Egypt and the Far East.

When we were back in Kansas City, the team and I worked at WDAF-TV (NBC), for free, just to keep our network formatting fresh. The News Director at WDAF was very receptive to getting another news crew for free and assigned us some great stories to cover.

Those two years became another broad base of experience for later use. I was promoted to Major, and was selected to go to Fort Leavenworth to attend the Command and General Staff College.

Big decision time!

Command and General Staff College, (C&GS), an intensive yearlong curriculum at Fort Leaven-worth, Kansas, was and still is, a guaranteed promotion to at least Lieutenant Colonel. Perhaps a star. No one has ever made general officer without graduating from there. Only the top 5% of Army Officers are selected to attend each year. I was very honored to be selected, but at the same time filled with mixed emotions about my future with the Army.

Knowing that I had done everything, broadcast wise, that I could do in the Army, and with three Bronze Stars, the Air Medal and combat command time, I knew that my next assignment after C&GS would most likely be a desk job. I made the decision to resign from active duty, and join the Army Reserves. I simply wanted to continue in television production and news.

Almost everyone thought I was nuts including my officer friends. They had never - and I mean never - heard of *anyone* turning down C&GS!

Lt. Col. Beatty, my commander at the News Center strongly advised me to reconsider. Even the two-star general, Major General Gordon Hill, the Army Chief of Information called the News Center in Kansas City and tried to talk me into going to C&GS. It was, without question, one of the biggest crossroads of my life.

I remember clearly the day I turned in my active duty military ID card for an Army Reserve card at Fort Leavenworth and put on my civilian suit.

That day I left a part of my life that literally had shaped and changed my life.

CHAPTER 9

"Fly, Try, and Tai"

*H*elping in the transition from military to civilian life were several friends, one of them Jim Sanders, of the U.S. Small Business Administration.

I was married again, and acutely aware of the lack of security, that the military paycheck provided each month. I guess you always know somewhere in your mind what it is you're going to be doing in the future, but sometimes things like security get in the way.

Looking back on "transitions in my life, I've found the easiest were the ones where I didn't stick my toe in the water to test it, but just leaped in. Now, that's not to say you do it blindly, but after a lot of research and weighing the pros and cons, it just doesn't make much sense to dabble in the decision making process.

I have to admit I dabbled after making the monumental decision to leave the Army. I accepted a position as Assistant Regional Administrator for Public Affairs for the U.S. Small

Business Administration. My offices were in Atlanta, and I was responsible for all public affairs activities for SBA's eight southeastern offices in Kentucky, Tennessee, North and South Carolina, Georgia, Alabama, Mississippi and Florida.

Any publicity good or bad, hurricane damages, floods, loans and other business stories I dealt with. I wrote press releases, did countless radio, television and newspaper interviews as well as advised each SBA State Director how to deal with positive and negative media encounters.

I found myself on the other end of the camera as the 'interviewee' rather than the 'interviewer'. I didn't know it then, but it was the best training I could have possibly received for teaching others how to respond to the media later on. I had now been on both sides of the camera.

It didn't take long for my broadcast instinct to surface. No one was really doing any national television programming aimed at the small business owner. The "Nightly Business Report" on PBS dealt with big business and the stock market and the major networks rarely gave more than a passing glance at small business stories, unless of course a scandal epoch proportions erupted.

I flew to Washington, D.C., with an idea and a format for a national television series entitled, "Small Business Journal". Fortunately for me, President Reagan had appointed an outside the box thinker in James Sanders, the SBA Administrator, and my friend.

He was very receptive to the idea, and told me to go ahead and produce a pilot program for the show. I went back to Atlanta absolutely ecstatic. I also had a Regional Administrator who was more than supportive. In my first year there, I managed to build a complete television studio in our regional office. We were the only region in the U.S. to have one.

The largest PBS program contributor in the south was located on the campus of the University of Georgia, in Athens, about an hour east of Atlanta, WGTV. I went there, literally with my hat in my hand, explained my concept and asked if they would produce the pilot program there. They were not only receptive, they jumped at the opportunity of being part of a new type of programming that would appeal to PBS stations around the country.

When the pilot was produced, I flew around the country to corporations lining up major contributors for the program so that we could begin the first year of programming. I made presentations in the boardrooms of some of this country's largest businesses that would view this program as an ideal vehicle to reach their small business markets.

I was wearing a lot of hats at this point, in addition to fulfilling my responsibilities as the Public Affairs Director for the eight southeastern states. I drove to Athens, Georgia at least once a week to work on production ideas, flew to Washington, D.C., about once a week to work out distribution and other details with PBS, and develop ideas for future programs.

I was in and out of the Atlanta airport so much that when I boarded my usual weekly flight for Washington one day, the flight attendant said, "Oh, you have that yellow tie on again. I like that one." You know you're flying too much when that happens!

God works major miracles at what seems like the strangest times. At the height of all of this activity, my wife and I decided to adopt a child! Why not? I was almost 38 and at a point where both my wife and I could really enjoy a child, and I missed being around Kelly and Kerry who were with their mother in Spokane, Washington.

When I was in Vietnam, an orphanage was close to our base camp, and whenever I could, I'd go over there with some goodies like candy bars and other things I knew the kids needed. I thought they were precious and they clung on to me whenever I arrived, just wanting some adult to give them some time and attention. I really enjoyed the moments I had with them.

When I started looking at places where we could adopt, I found out that Korea had a large need for adoptive parents, and would allow immigration to the U.S. We looked into Korea, found an agency and soon were on the list of waiting parents. In the meantime, we'd gone through the exhaustive home studies by the agency to see if we were going to be fit parents.

"Better have milk in the fridge, rather than beer", I said. We passed.

About 4 months later, we received a picture in the mail from the Korean agency. It was a picture of a 5-month-old Korean girl who was up for adoption. "This could be our daughter", I told my wife. "She's over there waiting for us". I took the little picture, a 4x5 as I recall, and went to the television studio and blew it up into an 11x14. Wow, she was really darling!

Less than a month later, we were on a flight to Korea. We were a couple of nervous 'about to be parents' going to pick up their child.

We arrived early in the morning and checked into the Hyatt Regency in downtown Seoul. The agency was expecting us, so I called to let them know we were there, and asked if we could come over and get our baby.

When we got there, Mr. Lee, the agency director went over all the paperwork we had to sign, and gave us the medical and adoption papers and then went to get our baby. He brought this tiny bundle out and handed her to me. Nothing could have taken that baby away from me now. Her name was Park Jung Me, but we had already named her Tai Ashley.

With papers and baby in our hands, we hailed a cab. This cab driver was an absolute terrorist, and it was rush hour in Korea, which is beyond nightmarish at its best. I could only imagine all of us being killed in a traffic accident in downtown Seoul.

We made it. I had noticed that Tai felt hot and was probably running a fever, and her little nose was running. As we walked down the hall to our room, a lady was unlocking her door right across from us. She inquired about the baby, and we said that we had just now adopted her.

She looked at Tai, and said, "It looks like she's got a little fever." She apologized and introduced herself. She was an American pediatrician visiting Korea! She said, take the baby into your room and I'll get my bag and be right over. Another miracle!

She examined Tai, pronounced her in good shape except for the fever and cold and gave us some medication for her that would clear it up, and at least make her comfortable on the long flight home. I wish I knew her name now, so that I could write to her and tell her that the "baby" she helped that night now has her Masters Degree in Education and is teaching in Kansas.

Before leaving Korea, the agency again confirmed that my wife and I were the ones who would be taking "several children" back with us to the States to their waiting parents who couldn't come over and get them. This was all arranged prior to our leaving the U.S., and we had agreed to do this.

Well, it wasn't "several children"; it was about 11, ranging in age from 6 months to 8 years old;

boys and girls. I have to tell you that we looked like Dr. and Mrs. Spock going through the Seoul International Airport with 11 little ones in tow!

Onboard the 747 for the long flight back, we were assigned a complete row of seats plus, near the back of the plane. We took turns going to the rest rooms changing diapers, getting water and having milk heated, and walking the babies up and down the aisles. The flight from Seoul to Los Angeles, at that time, was about 15 hours. Exhausting for anyone, but with 11 babies, an endurance test!

On one of my trips up and down the aisle, a lady got up from her seat and politely asked, "How many children do you have, sir?" I told her that my wife and I had just adopted one little girl and were bringing 11 others back to their new parents in the states.

She got the biggest smile on her face. She said, "Well, you just go back and sit down. I'm with a visiting nurses program, and there are 10 of us on this flight, and we'll take it from here, ok?" I'm pretty sure I saw a halo appear above her head.

We stopped in Los Angeles and Salt Lake City on the way to Atlanta. The adoptive parents met us in those three cities, and we delivered their precious bundles to them. I felt like a pediatrician myself! I think I took about a weeks worth of leave when we reached Atlanta, as much to get rid of the jet lag as getting used to having a baby around the house again. Tai was and is a blessing to us.

I have to tell you a funny story. My wife and I are both Caucasians. Tai, is of course, Asian, has black hair and didn't look anything like either one of us. Now anyone with a lick of sense would know that she's adopted, right? But, you can't imagine the number of people who would come up to us and say, "Is she adopted?" Hard to believe, I know.

One day, Tai was riding in her usual position, in the upper basket of the grocery-shopping cart that my wife was pushing, with me walking in front. As we got to the check out line, the lady in front of us looked back and said in a loud voice, "Oh, is she adopted?" I guess I'd had it with that question, and before thinking about it, I blurted back, "No M'am, we had her while we were in Korea." I think the lady about fainted, and the guy behind us lost it.

Children are little miracles, and we learn so much from them. As I'm going to talk about in Chapter 19, "Kids Letters to Terrorists", we need to listen to them so that we can learn how to communicate clearly all over again – before we're "cut out of the herd" by the media for an interview.

CHAPTER 10

"Being Cut Out Of The Herd"

*A*s I mentioned, I think we were really much better communicators as children. We weren't always politically correct, but we said things like we saw them - like they were. There was no mistaking what the message was.

But, as we grew up, we created this "box" to be in. It was a safe place. When we ventured out of the box, the teacher would say, "We don't do that in school", or our parents would say, "We don't do that in public", or heaven forbid, we would dress differently from anyone else at a certain period in our lives.

The "box" or "envelope" we created for ourselves provided us not only security, but somewhere to go when we didn't want to face events. The analogy I use is it's like being "cut out of the herd".

I rode cutting horses on ranches as a kid, and later as an adult in the NCHA (the National Cutting Horse Association), and the ABRA (the

American Buckskin Registry Association), cutting horse competitions.

In the cutting horse arena, you have to work 2 cows in 2½ minutes. You slowly ride toward the herd from one end of the arena to the opposite end where about 30 head of cattle have been all settled down along the back fence, and where they now feel safe.

You start the 'cut' by quietly entering the herd and bringing part of the herd away from the back fence and out with you toward the center of the arena. As you continue, this group begins to separate and return to the back fence – the "box" where they feel safe, until there is only one cow left out there.

At that point, this last cow turns around and looks at you and the horse and in desperation, tries to get back to the herd. It is your job to keep him from getting there. I'd give my horse all the loose reins he needed, and then would "sit on my pockets" and let him work.

I've always said at that point when the horse takes over, you are then riding a 1,100-pound border collie! You just happen to have the best seat in the house.

In competition, you have to cut a minimum of 2 cows in 2½ minutes. The only time you and your horse can get off a cow is when it gives up and turns away. Then you go back into the herd and bring out another one.

You see, that last cow out there knows instinctively that it's prey. And, what happens to prey? They get eaten! The cow didn't read about this or have 'herd meetings'. Millenniums of instinct and genetic transference take over and the cow reacts.

I've often felt like that last cow out there represents how many of people feel when they're "cut out of the herd" by the media in a crisis event and are asked to respond. People also feel like prey at times like that. The first instinct in many cases is to get back to the herd, or the box, our safety zone - the office.

It also emotionally defines the number one fear that people have - public speaking. Death is number three! I don't remember what number 2 is, but I suspect it's an IRS audit.

And then when we do respond, without this kind of media response training, the words that come out of our mouths don't really form the message we would like to have said. How many times have you listened to someone responding through the media and then asked yourself - "What did he just say?"

And, when you're busy applying filters to your message, such as "Is this a career ending statement I'm about to make?" or, "What will my peers think?"; "I'm going to sound stupid!"; "What if I don't know the answer ?", your body language is giving you away. Take time to look around you and see what's really happening and then remove yourself from the fray, listen to the question and just answer it honestly. The reason the media is coming to you is that you are the expert. You already have the answer, and sometimes don't know it. The more educated you are, the more you are apt to 'over-think' an answer.

Your audience already knows you're smart. They see your title and position below your picture. They want to know if you care.

In fact, people accept ideas from people they like, and reject equally good ideas from people they dislike. And, it has *nothing* to do with the idea. It has everything to do with how the idea was presented.

87% of what people get from you on television is body language. Throw away, taste, touch and smell and you're left with hearing. Hearing accounts for only 7% of your message! In other words, people are listening with their eyes first and then their ears. If they like what they see, they'll listen to what it is you have to say. It's really just that simple.

Information Gathering - The 5 Senses		
.........1. %	Taste	
.........1.5%	Touch	87% of your audience
.........3.5%	Smell	will determine your
.........7. %	Hearing	credibility by body
.........87.%	Seeing	language alone!

CHAPTER 11

"Small Business Journal"

*A*fter settling down with Tai in Atlanta, and getting back into my frequent flyer routine, I received a call from my boss, SBA Administrator, Jim Sanders. He asked me to stop by his office next week so that he could visit with me.

In addition to my television program, "Small Business Journal", which was being aired nationally on many PBS stations, I had also created a nationally syndicated radio program, called "Making it in Business", which was carried on numerous radio stations around the country. I was, in effect, a full time broadcaster, both on radio and television and still doing my public affairs job for the SBA.

When I arrived in Washington, D.C., that week, I went to the Administrator's Office, and his secretary told me he was in a meeting over at the White House, and asked me to meet him there. I walked over to the gate at the West Wing, and the guard took my credentials and checked the approved list for entry and found my name.

As I was walking up the curved driveway, I saw Jim coming out of the West Wing. He waved at me and we stopped, shook hands and I made some remark about how important that meeting must have been to be held in the West Wing.

He and President Reagan were good friends from California, and I knew he went over to the White House frequently

He said, "Have you been in the Oval Office?"

I replied, "No, I've only been on the "tourist side."

He said, "Come on, I'll take you in."

We walked back inside the West Wing, and past the Secret Service, and around the circle leading to the Oval Office.

The Secret Service agent standing outside the curved door to the Oval Office acknowledged Jim, as Jim said casually, "I'm just taking a friend of mine into the Oval Office." Just like you'd say, "My friend and I are going to lunch, ok?"

I have to admit, I'm a history buff, and am impressed not so much with people as I am with historic surroundings, places and events. When Jim opened the door to the Oval Office and ushered me inside, I could literally feel the history in that inner sanctum.

It wasn't as big as I thought. But, there it was, the desk and chair, the Presidential Seal rug, the rocking chair and couch. Jim left me alone there as he talked with the Secret Service Agent at the door. It was one of the strangest sensations I've ever had.

What if the President came in from the other side through *his* door? What would I say; "Just looking, Sir". "How are you anyway?" "I'm sorry my 'tang is all toungled up'." I looked around, and out the windows to the South Lawn, and around the room where so many decisions that literally changed the course of history have been made. It was a moment to say the least.

As we walked back to the SBA headquarters, Jim proceeded to knock me off my feet for the second time that day. He offered me a Presidential appointment. He asked if I would become the Assistant Administrator for the SBA for Public Affairs.

It had the magnitude of the decision I made turning down Command and General Staff College and leaving the military. I asked if I could think about it and talk to my wife, as it would mean a full 'redeployment' to Washington, D.C. He said, "Of course, but I need an answer this week."

I already knew what my answer would be: No. But, I wanted to savor the high mountain air of just being asked for a little while. Serving at the pleasure of the President is really not what I wanted to do in terms of security, with a new baby and a house mortgage. I knew by the end of this term, there was going to be a new President and therefore a new person selected for the position Jim had just offered me.

I called back later in the week, and we had a long talk, which concluded with my reasons for not accepting the appointment. He then asked if I would consider an appointment as SBA's National Director for Radio and Television, and move anywhere I would like in the country. Since it wasn't a Presidential appointment, and there was security attached, I gratefully accepted.

My wife was from Kansas City, and I had grown to like that city during the time I had been stationed there with the U.S. Army Television News Team. And, since I would have 96 District Offices around the country to serve, Kansas City made geographic sense, as it was centrally located. So, we moved back to the Midwest, and I was now the National Director of Radio and Television for the entire agency.

For the next year, I met myself coming and going, producing the television and radio programs, and going to Washington, D.C., for meetings and productions in the studios there. "Small Business Journal" was a success, to the point that we received a call from "The Nightly Business Report", also a PBS program, to see if we would be interested in merging some of our program elements. It was just a preliminary call, but signaled success to me.

When in Washington, I always made it a point to drop by the Administrators office and say hi to Jim. One day he asked me to sit down in his office with him and have a cup of coffee. I clearly recall the conversation. It went something like this:

"Dick, I'm going to abolish our job."

"What?" I replied.

He said, "Look, you don't belong in government and you know it. You're a broadcaster, a newsperson and an entrepreneur. You love radio and television. Take the program you created, 'Small Business Journal' and take it private. It's yours. Don't worry about being a success. You already are. Just do it. Trust me. I'm going to be leaving after President Reagan's term is up, and I don't want you left here."

I always respected Jim. He was a self-made man, a millionaire I'm sure, and a consummate entrepreneur. It was another one of those "jump in the pool" times, and I did. And I remained in contact with Jim in the years that followed, and he was right. Again, if you're passionately committed to something, it usually works.

I took the program private, produced, directed, anchored and did some of the feature reporting for the next several years. It was a great experience.

Also, during that time I started American ProVideo Productions, (APV). In the early 80's, video production was just beginning to emerge as the way to train, market, promote and educate the public. Corporations, associations, industry and educational institutions were starting to integrate video into their organizations. In Kansas City, APV was one of the first video production houses to open.

We produced programs for Hallmark, Burlington Northern, Yellow Freight, the American Academy of Family Physicians, AT&T, and a host of other businesses and organizations. I was elected President of the Kansas City Chapter of the International Television Association.

I gradually let "Small Business Journal" run its course, as I couldn't sustain a growing video production corporation and a PBS program at the same time, and still have any family life.

But, I also returned to my love of teaching, and as I mentioned in the Forward, my seminar started to take off. I never advertised it. It just seemed to have legs of its own, and the more sensational the reporting, the more demand there was for someone to help executives master television, radio, print, as well as public appearances.

In a small production company you do everything, from writing scripts, to lighting, make up, directing, shooting, editing, being 'on-camera' talent, doing voice-overs, and working with clients. You get the broadest experience possible.

The 80's flew by!

CHAPTER 12

"Tara"

I got a little ahead of myself in the last chapter. Let me catch you up on another big development in my life at that time. Her name is Tara. Originally, Kim Sung Hee. Also Korean.

In 1982, just before the monumental decision not to accept the Presidential appointment as Assistant Administrator for Public Affairs for the SBA, and prior to our move back to Kansas City, we decided to adopt another girl. Why not? Life was again in turmoil, and it just seemed like the thing to do, right? So, we decided to again adopt from Korea.

There is something about girls that's just plain magic. They have you wrapped around their little fingers from day one, and they know it, and so do you. And, there is nothing you can do about it!

The second adoption was much easier. Just an updated home study was practically all that was needed. They judged that Tai was about as well adjusted as they come, and could say McDonalds with the same authority as any kid at age 4.

We received Tara's picture in the mail from the same agency in Korea. She was so tiny! And cute! Instead of being 5 months like Tai, she was only 12 weeks old. We couldn't go personally to Korea again, so she was escorted back to us.

There are flight attendants in this country who are so caring and thoughtful. On their days off – they fly! They fly over to Korea and other places and pick up babies destined for parents around the U.S., and bring them back. I think they are extraordinary people!

All of our friends joined us at the Atlanta airport and we waited at the gate for Tara's arrival. Another 'right on time' delivery. Off she came all bundled up in a blanket with just her face sticking out being carried by an off duty flight attendant.

I often wonder what Tara thought when she arrived here. We took her right away to friend's houses where we all met and talked about her. Here she was in a foreign country, being held by strange people talking a different language than anything she had heard, and yet she seemed to sense that we loved her a bunch. So did Tai!

Tai had a little sister to take care of, and Tara had a big sister to try to emulate. Tara is, as of this writing, finishing her degree at the University of Kansas, with majors in English, Creative Writing and Art, and plans on also getting her

Masters Degree and becoming a teacher. I'm blessed to have both of them as daughters and I've learned a lot about me through their eyes.

Me and my driver, John Housenetch – "Groundhog"
in Cat Lai, Republic of Vietnam, 1967.

Me and one of our boats that we ran the jungle rivers
in, south of Saigon, 1967

Receiving my second Bronze Star from the 199ᵗʰ Light
Infantry Brigade Commander,
Brigadier General Shedd, 1968

Reporting on the de-mining of
the Suez Canal – Egypt 1974

I was Commander of Troops for the change of
command in Vietnam's XXIV Corps, June 1970.
Passing in Review. Left to right: Lt. Gen James
Sutherland, Captain Brundage, Lt. Gen Melvin Zais,
General Creighton Abrams, the
Army Chief of Staff.

On the set of my program, "Small Business Journal"
that aired on PBS stations around the country. 1980

Doing a stand up for "Small Business Journal", 1983

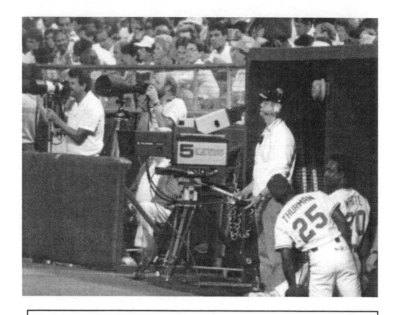

Running network camera #5 during a Kansas City
Royals game national telecast. My father can be seen
seated just below the 5 on the camera. 1987

Anchoring "Healthcare Business Review", a series of nationally syndicated television programs - 1995

Two of our cutting horses. Left: "Lucky Boon Fox"
Right: "Tari Watch"

"Normie" – named after the steer in the movie,
"City Slickers". Lesson: never name anything
you might eat. 1997

My buckskin cutting horse, "Ima Smok'n Janie" and I right after winning Reserve World Champion - 1994

CHAPTER 13

"The Reconnect"

*I*n the early 90's, when I owned American Pro-Video Productions, I directed a series of programs for News Line, an organization that produced daily newscasts for national associations during their conventions around the country.

The programs were aired in that convention city in all the major hotels, as well as the shuttle busses running to and from the convention center. I provided all the cameras, production equipment and crews and directed the programs. I later anchored the programs called, "Shuttlevision".

One series of programs we produced was for the American Academy of Pediatricians at their annual convention in Dallas, Texas. One of our first shoots was the keynote address and the speaker was Dr. Fred Rogers - most people knew him then as "Mister Rogers" - from the long running PBS program, *"Mister Rogers Neighborhood"*.

We lost a national treasure in 2002, when "Mister Rogers" passed away. He literally raised several generations of children through his PBS program, and was probably the kindest man I've ever met. In person, he was just like he appeared to be on the "Neighborhood." He had his Doctorate of Divinity Degree, was a Presbyterian minister, and an Honorary Diplomat in the American Academy of Pediatricians.

He stood up there at the podium for his keynote speech in his khakis' and sweater - just like on the "Neighborhood", and you expected at any moment to see "Mr. Postman" come out of the wings. He was talking to about 2,500 men and women pediatricians in the audience.

The huge grand ballroom was packed for his address, but you could have heard a pin drop, as "Mister Rogers" quietly talked to this select group of physicians about kids. It wasn't what he was saying exactly, although he was using the simplest of words to describe the wonderful service these pediatricians provide, it was *how* he was saying these things. It was as if he was talking to kids on his program, and this audience was mesmerized.

I swung the camera around the get some 'head' shots of these doctors listening to his speech so that I would have some "B-Roll" to edit with later on. As I zoomed I saw more than a few doctors with tears streaming down their cheeks.

What Fred Rogers was doing hit me like a thunderbolt. That moment was like being back home in the high country of Montana and breathing air after a lightening strike close by: Crystal clear, clean and fresh.

Dr. Rogers was "reconnecting" those physicians with the real reason they became pediatricians in the first place - because they love kids! And, they love *well* kids. And, they had forgotten.

Through all their medical school trials, exams, state boards, internships, residency programs - all the things they had to do to become doctors - they had forgotten the real reason they became pediatricians.

In his own inimitable style he was gently, quietly reconnecting them and giving them a new way to see their profession as others see them, and more importantly perhaps, as they once saw it so clearly themselves. What a wonderful affirmation of choice!

I've never forgotten that moment in time, and so many times since then I've looked out at audiences I'm speaking to, wondering how many have also lost their way, and in so doing are unable to communicate as well as they would like.

I try to reconnect all of my seminar participants with the reason they are doing something. When people make that connection, they are able to communicate so much clearer, not only in crisis situations, but also in their everyday lives by communicating that passionate commitment to their chosen fields.

Being passionately committed to what you're doing is contagious. Remember those early school years when you would come home and say to your parents, "I'm going to love math this year!" No you're not. You're going to love the way Ms. Elliott teaches it. On that first day, that teacher clearly revealed her passion for that subject and made you want to learn it.

That teacher created an image in a very short period of time. I ask my participants to give me their definition of "image". "What exactly *is* "image"? I get responses that range from, "What other people think about you" to, "The picture you project to other people." Two completely different answers. Neither is wrong even though they are exactly opposite definitions.

Here is my definition of "image":

"The first words out of your mouth, combined with the way you 'look' when you say them, and what people already know about you is your image. You will not change it."

In television you create your "image" often before you speak. In the electronic media, radio and television, your audience has to know *who* you are and *why* you're important to the story *before* you speak.

In a newspaper story, the reader can go back and identify again the person who is being quoted, but not in radio and television. Your image is cemented in the first few seconds in something we call "face time".

A newspaper story might read, "The tornado developed right on top of us last night with little or no radar warning possible", said Phil Clark,

Chief Meteorologist for the National Weather Service in a media briefing held earlier today.

The same story for the electronic media, radio and television might be aired like this. Looking at Phil Clark on the podium, we see him talking, but the audio is the newscaster who is saying, "At a media briefing held earlier today, Phil Clark, the National Weather Service's Chief Meteorologist commented on how rapidly last night's storm developed.

Now, they cut to both the audio and video Phil Clark as he says, "The tornado developed right on top of us last night with little or no radar warning possible."

The difference is very important from an "image" standpoint. In the electronic version, we are seeing Phil Clark before he speaks, and as his title and introduction are being aired; we are instantly forming an image of him. We've decided whether or not we like him, and whether or not we're going to believe what he has to say *before he opens his mouth.*

It's almost impossible to put a good face on bad facts, but if you're passionately committed to your calling, you're going to be credible even in the most serious crisis. "Face time" is extremely important.

When people were asked in a survey some 25 years ago what qualities they wanted in their national leaders, they were asked to list their "top 10". The results were astounding. Number one on the list was "honesty". Number two was "compassion". "Understanding issues of the times" was number 10!

Another extraordinary result of a survey conducted in the late '90's, found that *the only significantly consistent characteristic found in world leaders was 'caring'.*

We've all seen respondents in critical situations that exhibited that special caring nature. It's powerful, effective and most of all credible, because it's human.

Humanize your organization in a crisis. Your organization is not a building or product. It is a group of people who share a series of common business or organizational issues and ideas. But, above all, they're people.

CHAPTER 14

"The 4 Instant Lessons"

*T*he tendency in a crisis is to pull away from the community and do damage control. The opposite re-action is the most powerful. Engage the community. Bring the community in with you.

There are four, what I call "Instant Lessons" for any media appearance. Here they are:

Name: (Cross it off - no one is going to remember your name.)

Organization: (Circle it: People will remember your organization.)

Said: (Cross it off - hardly anyone will remember what you said.)

Liked: (Circle it. People will remember whether or not they liked you.)

You should now have only two words circled: Organization and Liked. Now draw a line connecting those two words. If you can walk away from a media interview with the audience liking you - you've won!

Let me prove it. How many times have you gone to work in the morning and said to a co-worker; "Did you see that guy from the FBI last night on the news? He was talking about.... oh, some case in Mississippi. I can't remember. But I'll tell you, he was sharp."

You walked away from that television interview liking the FBI. You didn't remember anything that was said, or for that matter the agent's name, but you liked him and therefore the organization.

Nowhere was the "likeability" point better illustrated than during the very first televised debate, Nixon vs. Kennedy.

In 1960, that debate was broadcast in black and white. In those days the cameras were not as sensitive as they are today, and we had to pour a lot of light on the subjects being taped.

Nixon refused make up. Kennedy used it, along with good body language. Nixon sat stiffly in his chair with his hands in his lap; while Kennedy had his bottom pushed back in the chair and leaned forward slightly using his gestures. Nixon, because he refused make up, was sweating. Kennedy used it and didn't.

What amazed the political handlers at that time was the difference between radio and television. Those who watched on television were convinced by a significant margin that Kennedy won. Those who listened on radio, and there were many in 1960 who did, were convinced by the same significant margin that Nixon won! Body language and being liked – the very essence of television.

It was at that moment in political history that the candidate's staffs realized just how important what you say with your body language was to the outcome of the debate. And, the rest is history.

Skip ahead 20 years to the debate between President Carter and his challenger, Governor Reagan, another extraordinary lesson in body language.

When I teach my seminar, I ask this question, and never once has a group failed to answer it correctly. Someone in the audience will remember. "What did Governor Reagan *do* at the end of the debate, not something he said, that swung thousands of undecided votes to Reagan?"

Someone will always remember that Reagan walked all the way across the stage to President Carter's podium and shook his hand. Hardly anyone remembers a word that was exchanged during the debate, but nearly everyone remembers that gesture.

And, so did thousands of undecided voters, for when a survey was taken from that group, that gesture - going over and shaking hands - was perceived as a very "nice thing to do". Body language not words won that debate. Your face, voice and gestures do more to convey the message of your sound bite than you can imagine.

I know that appearing on television, or radio, or talking with newspaper reporters is not a major part of your daily routine. But, when you do face the media, you should know the arena you are about to enter, and you must know exactly how to *perform* in it. Your *presence* is critical to both you and your organization's success.

Put another way, with each appearance on television for example, you will reach more people than you will be able to shake hands with personally the rest of your life. And, you'll do it in mere seconds.

People say they don't watch a lot of television, but they do. In fact, a recent survey suggests that 67 percent of the American public gets 100 percent of their daily information from television. I don't know about you, but I think that's a little frightening considering the 'state of television news'.

What it really says, is that we are not reading about those things that affect our lives as much as we probably should, and many times people simply accept as fact those reports they see on the evening news.

CHAPTER 15

"Why do we watch 'danger'?"

I always ask my seminar audiences, "Why do you suppose we watch danger on television? Overturned tanker trucks on fire, automobile wrecks and the other havoc the media traffics in so heavily?"

Do you think we wanted to watch the World Trade Center Towers come down a thousand times? Why did we continue to watch? What is it that compels us to stay tuned to these crisis events?

Is it because we're curious? Is it because we can say, "There but for the Grace of God go I?" Maybe it's voyeuristic? Or, is it somehow morbidly exciting? You can't imagine the answers I get in my live seminars to that one!

I think there is a medical explanation for this. My premise is this: *We simply cannot look away from danger.* And here's why.

I believe we arrived at the top of the food chain on this earth by intelligent design. Our brains are programmed to not only intercept danger signals but to give them the highest priority.

The body of knowledge in neuroscience has doubled in the past few years. In the relatively new field of neurocardiology many new networks that transmit information to the brain have been discovered, including those in the heart.

One of the most fascinating for me is located at the base of the brain, the reticular activating system (R.A.S.). The R.A.S. connects with major nerves in the spinal column and the brain. It sorts the millions of impulses that reach the brain each second, sending the trivial, or unimportant off into space, but letting the vital through to put us on alert.

This part of the brain, located at the top of the spinal cord, has evolved over the eons with a strong inherent tendency to *magnify* negative incoming messages and *minimize* positive ones.

This certainly protected us from dangers long ago, and still functions today in almost every environment. Let's suppose that everything has gone quite smoothly at work today. Many good things have happened. During the day, one of your managers made a very small negative comment - nothing significant at all. But, what do you think about on the way home? All the good things that happened, or that one small seemingly insignificant comment?

We concentrate on the negative because it represents danger. Not in the life threatening way our ancestors were threatened by physical dangers, but in new ways. In an increasingly complex business world there are dangers lurking that could end a career, or at the very least prevent a promotion, cause financial chaos or affect our family lifestyles.

Gastroenterologists tell us that the first place a signal is sent is to the gut. This is the "second brain" located inside our intestines, or the "enteric nervous system".

According to Michael D. Gershon, M.D., Chair of the Department of Anatomy and Cellular Biology at Columbia University College of Physicians and Surgeons, this system is independent of *and* interconnected to the brain.

Remember when you or someone you know had a gut reaction to something? Did you ever hear someone say, "Trust your gut"? We need to listen to our guts.

The very next place the events information is transmitted to and from is probably the heart. Neurocardiologists have discovered a complex "heart brain" and say that heartbeats are anything but the simple act of pumping blood around our circulatory system.

The heart's electromagnetic field (EMF) is the most powerful produced by the body, and is said to be approximately 5,000 times more powerful than the field produced by the brain. According to *The*

American Journal of Cardiology, the electrical changes in "feelings" transmitted by the human heart can be felt and measured at least five feet away!

In short, our hearts are actively, not passively, seeking information from one another. How many times have you heard someone say, "She has a good heart"? Or, "His heart is just not in his work." We've heard these kinds of statements long before we knew anything about neuro-cardiology.

That is why I think that someone who genuinely responds with honesty and compassion during a crisis is the most powerful and credible person at that time.

Through all these body systems and perhaps many more that will be discovered later, we are able to discern more about an individuals response in terms of its truthfulness, credibility and completeness than we are able to think about consciously.

That, in my opinion is at the very heart of every response we make. Quit over-thinking your responses! The answer is right there, in your heart, your gut and your innate ability to make the right response. If in doubt, go back and re-read the chapter "Where else would the elk be?"

Robert Frost, the poet, had it right. "The brain is a wonderful thing", he wrote. "It starts to work the moment you get up in the morning and does not stop until you get to work." I often think of it in these terms; "It doesn't stop until you get in front of a reporter!"

It's also important to understand *why* we watch what we watch on television, hear on radio or read in newspapers so that we can respond with some kind of proper perspective.

I don't think news directors have gotten it yet. People who conduct focus groups to find out what programs people watch, not *want* to watch, put a number of people in a room, each with a monitor and a remote control. They are told to watch the monitors, and if they don't like what they are watching to change channels until they find one they like.

Unfortunately for all of us consumers of programming, I think the wrong programs are being aired because of a belief by those who choose them that this is what we *want* to watch.

It's exactly the opposite in my opinion! It's not that we *want* to watch murder, rape and robbery stories, it's that *we cannot look away!* We are evolutionarily programmed *not* to look away from danger.

Let me give you an exercise to do to prove the point about not being able to look away from danger. You probably drive the same route to and from work each day, right?

Let's say there is a slow down today, and traffic is backed up where it normally flows along smoothly. You pull over slightly to the right so that you can see down the road, and spot a patrol car with its lights on and two cars in front that were obviously involved in a minor fender-bender.

Nothing unusual. You look at all the other drivers in front of you and think, "Get going and stop the gawking, it's only a fender-bender". But, what happens when you get up there? Do you look or drive by with your eyes straight ahead? I know the answer and so do you. You simply *cannot* avoid looking because it represents danger.

The next time this happens, I challenge you to drive completely past the incident without once even glancing over. I'll bet you can't do it!

I think news departments in local stations would like to cover more news, but are caught in this cycle of mayhem and the ever-present theme, "If it bleeds it leads". I sometimes relate news to emails; spam, spam, spam, mildly interesting, spam, spam, spam.

Newscasts today are faster, slicker, edited with sound effects and scenes that are intended to elicit an emotional response from the viewer. They simply won't or can't deal with complex issues.

News today is a huge business. Ratings equate to dollars, and the more audience a news program can draw, as measured in ratings points, the more the station can charge for commercials. One ratings point nationally equates to nearly a million television households, and that equates to money.

There are so many shows out there today that look like news, sound like news, have anchors and reporters, but are they news? Is there a blurring distinction between what is news and what is entertainment? I think so.

The late Fred Friendly, CBS news president, and really the father of television news, was once quoted as saying, "Poor television is so lucrative, it is now economically impossible to do good television."

Although studies suggest that violent crime is actually down in many cases, the *reporting* of violent crime is up by a large percentage.

The people who are responsible for providing balance to the news are not the news people; they are the people in professions and industry who are being interviewed. You! There is such a rush to headlines today, that knowing how to respond and provide that balance and give an audience the proper perspective on a story is not only a nice to know skill, it may be critical to your continued success.

There is another element, especially in television that prevents much of the coverage we would like to see. Television is "visual", and it's very difficult to point a camera at a school bond issue. It's much easier to point that camera at an overturned tanker truck on fire. And remember, that overturned tanker truck on fire represents "danger".

The end result is that we are not being fed news, but what I call "distractions". There simply aren't the investigative pieces being done that would most certainly educate and inform the public about the world in which we live.

If that is true, then there is obviously a need to learn how to respond during crisis events. The media will be there, and often are "first responders".

I've often heard someone say in the audience, "Oh, I don't speak to the press. That's not my job. We have a PIO who does that." That doesn't work very well today. If you're on the scene of any crisis, it doesn't make any difference to the media if you're the PIO or not.

And, for you to say "No comment" is simply not an option. I tell my clients that "No comment" means you're guilty. At the very least a "No comment" remark gives the impression that you may be hiding something. Or, why else wouldn't you comment?

Everyone in your organization needs to be trained to respond, even if only to get the media to the right person. There is a tremendous difference between saying, "No comment", and "Of course, we'll give you all the information we can. Please come in and let me get our spokesperson for you."

Common sense? Of course.

CHAPTER 16

"The Royals"

*O*wning a video production company, I did a multitude of programs from 1984 to 2000, ranging from broadcast, commercials, corporate and industrial programs.

Since Kansas City is a major league city with the Kansas City Royals baseball franchise and the Kansas City Chiefs football team, some of us in video production were often asked to crew for the network productions.

Since I was also teaching my seminar, the first being in 1980 in Anchorage, I was always looking for things that I did in production work that would cross over and become teaching points in my seminar. One was with the Kansas City Royals.

In about 1986, the season after the Royals had won their 'miracle' World Series against the St. Louis Cardinals in that unforgettable game in KC, I got a call from a sports network crewing service asking me if I would like to run one of the cameras at Royals Stadium for the network games. I was a diehard Royals fan and leaped at the opportunity. I worked virtually all of the camera positions, but the one I liked the most was "camera 5" which was right in the Royals dugout.

I got to know George Brett, Bo Jackson, Brett Saberhagen, Frank White, and the rest of the team over many, many games in the next 5 years. I did this in addition to doing programming for "NewsLine" and the other video productions for my own corporation.

The operation of each camera during a live broadcast is an orchestrated symphony directed from the tractor-trailer van parked outside the stadium. There are specific assignments that each camera has, and you listen to the director in one side of your headset, and the announcers in the other side. Sometimes it could become deafening! And confusing.

On camera 5, since it was right inside the Royals dugout, I had a number of responsibilities. I would cover all right handed batters because they faced me, all left handed pitchers for the same reason, and all steals from 1st to 2nd base as well as pick off attempts on 1st base.

Watching baseball on television can be laborious, but actually putting together a broadcast is a very fast moving series of events, to include the 'instant replays'.

Away from the stadium doing news, I can remember my cameraman telling me that he always kept both eyes open - one looking in the viewfinder - and the other checking the periphery. I did the same at the ballpark.

For example, if I had a runner on 1st base, a left-handed pitcher and a right-handed batter, I was a very busy guy. If the director had me cover the 1st base runner, I had to keep the other eye scanning what that right-handed batter was going to do. Because, if he squared up to bunt, I knew I either had to get the bunt or the 'steal' to 2nd base.

All of this happened in seconds. You could hear the director saying, "Ready 5 on the batter, ready 5 – take 5". You had about 3 seconds to frame the shot and get it in focus and follow the action.

Directors get rather upset when that doesn't happen, and one side of your headset tends to become more profane than the 'broadcast' side.

The point here, and I apologize to the readers for belaying this for so long, is simply this. A cameraman who has you framed during a television news interview in a "60 minutes" shot, e.g., just your head, is doing the same thing I was doing at the ballpark: He is also looking with the other eye at what your gestures are saying.

The minute he sees you using your gestures, he *must* pull back and frame the shot to include the gestures. Gestures simply tell the rest of the story.

Visuals *are* the story, 87% to be exact, and the use of proper gestures dramatically adds to the story.

I can't tell you how many times during a pre-interview with someone, before the camera is turned on, they will say, "What do you want me to do with these?" - meaning their hands.

I usually reply, "What do you normally do with them?"

They'll reply, "I can't talk unless I use my hands".

"Great", I'll say, "use them."

But, invariably, as soon as the camera rolls, they produce what I call the "fig leaf" (hands in front of their groin), or they put them behind their backside.

In either case, those hands don't have a chance to add to the story. They suddenly have no idea why they grew those appendages, but they are not going to use them!

Using your gestures not only adds to the story, it almost always insures that you won't be tightly framed in a head shot with just your face showing.

Cameramen are only as good as their last story just as reporters are, and they are not going to miss 87% of the story – the visuals – by not loosening the shot to capture the gestures.

Once you've developed your themes, practice them to include the use of gestures. Using your gestures also helps to loosen your face. You'll learn more about "themes" and how to develop them and how they fit into the overall story in Chapter 21, "The Winning Game Plan".

CHAPTER 17

"The Biggest Fear"

*I*n the first few minutes of my seminar, I invariably ask my audience, "What's your biggest fear about being interviewed by the media"? I wait patiently for about 10 seconds as no one wants to be the first to speak. Remember, public speaking is the number one fear.

Then, I remind them that the invitation they got to attend this seminar said it would be highly interactive and you don't even have to raise your hands. After that, things loosen up and learning begins.

In response to my question about your biggest fear, I hear such things as "I'm going to look stupid". "I'm going to get brain freeze". "I'm afraid I'm going to make a 'career ending' statement". "They're going to ask me a question I don't have the answer for." "They're going to make me look bad." Etc., etc., etc. All of those answers I hear about the biggest fear, but at some point, someone will say, *"They're going to take me out of context"*. Yes, they are. And, yes, that's the biggest fear I hear from seminar participants almost anywhere I teach in the world.

And why are they going to take you out of context? Not because their agenda is different from yours, even though in many cases, it is. Not because they want to make you look bad or any of the dozens of other reasons I hear. It's because you - yes you - talk too long! And, that is a reporter's worst nightmare.

Not only that you'll talk too long, but you'll talk in your own jargon that may be understandable to you and others in your select group, but not to the reporter or the general public.

The reporter is standing there with a microphone in your face, and do you know what's going through that reporters mind? I can tell you because I've been there.

The reporter is thinking, "I'm going to have to go back to the station and stand in line in front of an edit booth." And there are never as many edit booths as there are reporters standing in line to use them because you talked too long!

It's your fault - not the reporters - that you've been taken out of context. You finish your inter-view and go home and watch the report on television and say, "Well, yes, I said that - but not that way!"

The reporter had to edit your soundbite into something like 8 seconds, so the editor took a little from the beginning and perhaps a little from the end, electronically edited them together, and voila, you've just been taken out of context.

During the interview, the reporter knows from the length of your response that he or she is going to have to edit, so after you leave the camera person turns the camera around and frames the reporters head nodding sagely for several seconds, called of course, "nod shots"

To cover the edit point, they simply edit in the nod shot for several seconds, carrying your audio underneath. Now it looks like a much more expensive two-camera operation, starting with you on camera and cutting to the reporter nodding sagely for several seconds while still listening to you and then cutting back to you for the conclusion.

To the viewer, this looks perfectly natural. To you at home watching the evening news, this can be a media disaster! I want to teach you how never to be taken out of context again. It's learning to speak simply and in sound bite format.

I think the term sound bite has gotten a bad rap in recent years because some of those who use a variation of the format distort it and don't answer the question. They simply use it for their own advantage and you see it used many times during political campaigns. But, used honestly and openly, it can be very effective, and prevents you from being taken out of context.

Most of us have simply not been taught how to talk in 12-second sound bites. The more educated people are the more they have to say, and the more they want the reporter to understand the issue at hand. They want to educate the reporter.

Reporters are coming to you - not for a career move - but to get a sound bite. They often have several stories each day to cover, and they are hoping that you will give them a sound bite they don't have to edit. And, if you do, they'll come back and use you as a resource time and again.

It takes practice to perfect brevity. Someone once said, "If you want me to talk for an hour, I'm ready now. If you want me to talk for 12 seconds, give me a week".

Many of my students say, "I don't think I can possibly tell them about this in 12 seconds."

But, by the time we're done with the daylong seminar, they not only can, many are hoping they run into someone from the media so they can try it!

CHAPTER 18

"The Ambassadorial Seminar"

*I*n the mid-90's, I received a call from the U.S. State Department asking if I would be interested in conducting the media response training for new U.S. Ambassadors prior to their taking their posts around the world.

I was not only interested, but also humbled by the phone call. I knew that some of the ambassadors were close personal friends of the President, and would be appointed. Others would be career diplomats who, having risen through the ranks with the highest of marks, would be elevated to the rank of Ambassador by the President. It would be a great mixture of people, business backgrounds and international intellect.

I was given the global areas that these new Ambassadors were to be stationed, and I prepared "case studies" that represented their potential worst nightmares should they happen. I used these during the seminar when I conducted one-on-one interviews in front of the cameras.

I asked if I should bring my camera as I usually do for my on-camera portion of the exercise, and the seminar coordinator said that we would be using the State Department television studios. This would give the new Ambassadors real experience in front of studio cameras.

I had these new Ambassadors for their final two days of their two-week orientation in Washington, D.C. They were given "country briefings" by CIA, and FBI, and met with Special Operations personnel at Fort Bragg, as well as their congressional delegations up on Capitol Hill. Learning how to respond to the media during times of crisis was my responsibility.

I did this three times over a period of several years, and made many lasting friendships in the process. Several of the Ambassadors invited me to their Embassies to teach their entire staffs, including the Embassies in Helsinki, Prague and Budapest, some several times.

I am always amazed at how simple the process of responding to the media is, and yet, even at the highest levels of government, it is not easily seen or used.

I received an email in the middle of the night from my friend, the Ambassador to Finland. She was preparing to give a major speech to an international organization the next day and asked if I would read it and get back to her with my suggestions.

I read her prepared remarks, and they sounded like a policy statement, not something she would say. The message was lost in diplomatic language, which wasn't necessary for this particular audience, and certainly not the way I'd heard her speak so eloquently from the heart before.

I emailed back several very succinct soundbites to her that contained themes that mirrored her own messages, but knowing her, would also be something she would say from her heart. She was, and is, an extraordinary person and a passionate speaker.

She wrote back to me and said, "Thank you from preventing me from giving a policy statement, and reminding me that the most powerful messages come from the heart – not the head. You are a treasure to those of us stationed around the world."

It's always nice to receive that kind of compliment. But, at the same time, I don't feel I teach anything extraordinary at all. Some have called it "new millennium thinking on how we all communicate", but I think of it simply as something we all did so well as children.

We marveled at things, and shared that joy with others, unashamed and unwilling to be put down by those who couldn't or wouldn't see the magic.

CHAPTER 19

"Kids' Letters to Terrorists"

*U*nfortunately we grew up. As I've mentioned, we communicated much better as kids. We
weren't always politically correct, but when we
got done talking, there was no doubt in anyone's
mind what we had just said. It was clear, concise
and from our hearts.

We hadn't yet developed our brains enough to
cloud issues with thoughts like, "Is this a career
ending statement I'm about to make?" "Am I
going to look foolish saying this?" "What will my
peers think when I utter this?" These thoughts
and many, many more shoot through our heads at
warp speed during a time of crisis when we are
called upon to respond. The real response is
already there. Simply let it out.

Right after 9-11, it seemed no one was talking
to children about what had just happened. Parents
didn't know how to talk to kids about terrorism,
and neither did schools. Kids wanted to know, and

they also had something to say, but no one was listening.

Two of my friends, John Shuchart and Steve Scearcy in Kansas City went to the Superintendent of Schools at a large school district there and asked if they could have kids write letters to terrorists? What would they say? What are their thoughts about what just happened to this country? What did they think about the people who committed these acts?

The results were impressive, and available in the book entitled "Kids Letters to Terrorists", Personhood Press.

Here are just two of the extraordinary letters these elementary kids wrote.

A boy wrote: *"All my friends are asking "why?" Not me. I understand the rage you feel. I understand the hopelessness you feel. I understood it all on 9-11. I am in the 8th grade and understand you cannot act on feelings of rage or live to promote hopelessness. I am a kid and know this, why don't you?"*

A girl wrote: *"You made it seem like its permanently cloudy. It feels like there could be a storm at any moment. I guess that's what you wanted right? I live in a state where there are lots of tornados. Every year we have to live though that season. Why did you want to make another 'season' for me to have to live through?"*

What powerful thoughts, and, from children in elementary school! What simple writing and yet so clear, moving and heart rending. No amount of adult editing, political touching up, or other changes from the mature world could make them any more powerful or succinct. We need to reconnect with messaging we learned as kids. We need to be so moved by what kids are saying that we actually listen to them and try to communicate with each other as they do.

My greatest pleasure is to look out at an audience and see the lights come on in their faces as they personally reconnect with *why* they are doing what they are doing with their lives. For many, it's the first time they've really thought about it, and for others it's confirmation that their professional decisions were the right ones, and they simply needed to enjoy it and pass on the passion to others.

Your ability to move others by communications is only limited by your willingness to open up and let people see how you really feel about the situation you are dealing with.

Look at the most recent examples of people achieving greatness through communicating from the heart. Before 9-11, Rudy Giuliani was a lame duck mayor of New York, recently divorced, and soon to be replaced. For those of us in the mid-west - no big deal.

After 9-11, he became the most sought after speaker on the circuit. Why? Because Rudy Giuliani spoke from his heart and for the first time in my life "humanized" New York.

New York was a city with people who hurt, who had paid the ultimate sacrifice trying to rescue others, who reached out to the rest of America and said thank you for helping. I never thought I'd see "I love New York" bumper stickers in Kansas, but there they were!

And there was Rudy. How difficult was it for him to take world leaders down to "ground zero" everyday? To see the destruction, the smell, the sights and sounds that reminded him of that horrible few hours on September 11th, 2001. But, he did it. He did it with dignity and you saw him cry. He became human in the eyes of the viewers, and at the same time became one of the most powerful people in America. Not through political manipulations, but through human compassion, caring and communicating from his heart about a city he loves.

There are obviously others who have come along and will in the future who will do the same thing. When we stop over thinking our responses, the logical human compassionate response will come out – it has to. It's been there all the time.

CHAPTER 20

"Buick, Gidget and Normie"

*I*n the early 90's, I decided to build a ranch house and indoor riding arena on 20 acres I owned just west of Kansas City. I had already returned to my love of horses, and in particular cutting horses, and was competing regularly on the circuit.

I found myself doing less video production and more seminars by the mid-90's. Technology was beginning to change in the video production business, and at the same time, broadcast news was becoming more sensational. I found clients were making their own transitions from outside video production services to internal computer driven presentations produced by their own personnel.

At the same time there seemed to be a marked increase in the number of organizations discovering the absolute need to be prepared for responding to the media, particularly in crisis situations. I was getting more requests for presenting my seminar then ever.

I had also done just about everything I'd ever wanted to do in broadcasting and video production work. Both had provided me not only with a good living, but a wealth of knowledge and stories about people and how they react in front of cameras.

And, all of it provided good solid content for my seminars. It was time for a change not only in the direction I wanted to take my professional life, but also in my leisure time.

I think, for me, life is a series of passages divided into chunks of about 8 years. Maybe there is some type of circadian rhythm imbedded in our evolutionary past. At least for me, I feel the need for some change in my life at those intervals.

I don't know why I feel the need to explain it, except for the fact that I watch other people who seem to have this focused direction in all aspects of their life and stay with that for a lifetime. I think I would become extremely bored.

I'm not talking about a change in vocation, but avocation. I feel the need to remain focused on the seminar and my interest in broadcasting, but I also like to do other things in my leisure time and try as best as I can to excel at them. One of those was cutting horse competitions.

From my early days on the ranch during those summers in Montana, my memories of cutting horses remain indelible. Extremely athletic, strong, durable, smart, and not easily spooked, the American Quarter Horse is a remarkable animal.

I also learned a lot about the "fight or flight" syndrome from these wonderful animals that I would talk about later on in my seminars. I don't think a horse ever purposely hurt anyone, but if you get them frightened and cornered, they'll react by fleeing, and if you happen to be in the way you are probably going to get run over.

Both of my daughters, Tai and Tara, also loved horses, but had never been around them. I wanted them to have that experience. Susan had grown up around horses in Leavenworth, Kansas.

Her mother had purchased a horse for her when she was in her early teens and she rode and cared for that horse until "Misty Morn" passed away at the old age of 31. For all of us, and particularly Susan, it was truly like losing a family member.

I think teenage girls bond with horses. Both instinctively respond to the flight or fight syndrome. Girls at that age become "prey", and boys at that age become "predators". I think that teenage girls identify with the prey animal and therefore bond with horses more than boys. Boys tend to want to "break" a horse and compete on them, while girls will bond with a horse and spend much more time making the horse a willing partner in whatever the event is.

Those emotions and intuitive behavior have a direct relationship on how we later respond to the media. Men are more action oriented, have a need for the bottom line, and talk from their heads, often hiding emotions. That translates to shorter responses and little or no discernable body language.

Women are more intuitive, talk from their hearts, and are more likely to use observable body language. Women, however, talk their way to the bottom line. That translates into longer responses.

There is a wonderful combination that must be made. Men - learn how to use your face and talk from your hearts. And women - learn how to get to the bottom line and still use that good body language.

On our 20 acres I designed our house so that when you opened the back door, you stepped into the indoor arena. Around the arena, which was about 150 feet by 80 feet, there were stalls, a tack room, feed room, wash racks and large remote controlled doors on either end of the arena to move cattle in and out for practicing cutting.

We also decided to raise two American Bison. I had heard that they were great to practice cutting on, as they were almost tireless, and tended to repeat the same pattern time and again. This would really help the horses learn how to trap a cow in the middle of the arena and work it there when we were in competition.

But, bison are *not* like cattle at all. They are stubborn, quite capable of going through the side of a building, have almost no respect for fences, horses or people. We didn't know this, of course.

We domesticated them as best we could and practiced on them in the arena while they were young.

We named the male "Buick", as I thought someday he would be about the size of a Buick, and the other, a female, we named "Gidget." She was cute in a shaggy sort of way. Both would come thundering across the large meadow in the back of barn when we'd come out in the evening with their grain. We had placed the bunk feeder for the grain some 100 feet from the barn, so when you were out there putting grain in the feeder you were pretty exposed.

It crossed my mind more than once, as they were approaching me at speeds of up to 30 miles an hour, "I sure hope they stop before getting to the grain bucket I'm holding!" They seemed to have two speeds – on and off.

We also fed about 15 head of cattle for a neighboring rancher in exchange for using them for cutting practice. We hadn't used the bison for months, and while getting ready for the World Show, I decided that I'd like to practice with my horse on "Buick" in the arena. He had grown quite a bit by then, and really wasn't fond of being herded anywhere, let alone being confined in the arena with a horse and rider.

I guess I still looked at him like the calf he once was. He looked at me like something he could easily take out. When Susan closed the arena gate, he took one look at my horse and me and immediately lowered his head and started pawing the ground.

We were about 20 seconds from being gored by what was now a very large bison. As calmly as I could, with my adrenaline at an all time high, I quietly said to Susan, "Open the arena door first, and then open that arena gate fast and get out of the way. Buick wants out now!"

Both doors were opened, and Buick apparently decided freedom in the pasture was the best course, and charged out of arena. That was the last time we had either of them in the arena. We sold them to a bison breeder who had railroad ties for fencing.

We also had one steer that we were taking care of for a friend of ours. I found out you never "name" anything that eventually is going to wind up on someone's dinner table. "Normie", named after the calf that Billy Crystal took care of in the movie, "City Slickers" became quite a pet. He'd come running up for his evening treats, and Susan would scratch his forehead and call him "knucklehead".

One day, Normie's owners, arrived and announced that Normie was ready for the dinner table. I, for one, did not see the golden arches forming on his back, but apparently they did. We bid our farewell to "knucklehead" as Susan fondly called him, and they put him in their trailer and off they went. We went in the house and pulled out his scrapbook with pictures. We didn't eat steak for about a month.

We all rode - Tai, Tara, Susan and I. Susan and I really got into cutting horse competitions.

Susan had grown up riding English and she and Misty Morn competed in all of those kinds of events, including jumping.

Once she got on a cutting horse, she was hooked. There is quite a bit of difference between English and Western riding. I'm pretty sure that horses really don't understand a lot of things we make them do, like polo for instance. But, they do understand working cattle.

The American Quarter Horse is adept at working cattle. They instinctively know how to move cattle and are easily trained to compete in cutting horse competitions. I explain this in Chapter 10, "Being Cut Out Of The Herd".

We fed horses and cattle before going to work, and the same in the evenings and rode everyday. On weekends we'd trailer the horses somewhere in the Midwest on Friday night. We'd get them bedded down for the night, get up early on Saturday and compete Saturday and Sunday and trailer them back to the ranch, feed and water everyone and get ready for work on Monday.

It was a great time in life, and I was probably in better condition during that period than at any time except perhaps during my early military experiences.

I'll never forget the people I met on the cutting horse circuit. Most of us grew up on or near ranches, and by the time we reached our mid life, we had the means and desire to get back to horses and compete with them.

You never really knew what your fellow competitors did for a living. We all dressed in wranglers, boots, spurs and chaps. Just like on the ranch. But, once in awhile business would creep its way into the mix.

One day, not long after the Oklahoma City bombing, we were in the middle of Kansas at a cutting horse competition and the pager I wore on my belt under my chaps went off. I carried a pager then as I was still doing occasional on-call production work for the networks as a cameraman. I owned my own camera gear, and often when there was breaking news, the networks would send their correspondent out to cover the event, and hire me to do the shoot.

My page that day was from NBC wanting me to meet their correspondent in Salina, Kansas, so that we could produce a story on the van that Timothy McVey had rented there that was used in the bombing.

I heard another pager going off several times on another cowboy who was also riding in the warm up arena with a group of us. He rode up alongside of me and said, "Who's paging you? What do you do?"

I replied, "I've got a video production company, and it's NBC wanting me to go to Salina, and shoot a story on the Ryder truck that McVey rented there. What do you do?"

He said, "I'm a Special Agent with the FBI and they want me to go out there too. Want to trade pagers?" Over the years, both Hank and I became friends and have laughed at that exchange many times.

I met many wonderful people who rode cutting horses, and found that people who love and care for horses are first class people with few hidden agendas. I suspect it really is about doing physical work, engaging in friendly competition, being with people who value the simple things in life. Whatever it is, it makes for wonderful times with great people.

Susan and I spent a lot of time with my trainer up in Nebraska, Larry Vance and his family. He was one of those quintessential cowboys who worked from sunup to sundown training his own cutting horses he would compete on, and a number of other horses for clients. He probably had 10 horses in training at his place at any given time, and he worked each one everyday, rain, snow or shine.

He had an indoor arena, but it wasn't heated, and he had to ride out and get the cattle out of the pasture and bring them to the arena. In the winter, in Nebraska, that can be a bone-chilling, windy chore. He'd just pull his Stetson down a little bit, wrap that silk scarf around his neck, put on his gloves and grab a handful of reins and get the job done. We did that several times with him, and he has my undying admiration.

Larry was also a AAA rated judge with the NCHA (The National Cutting Horse Association), and when he wasn't training a string of cutting horses at his ranch in Inavale, Nebraska, he was flying around the country judging competitions.

He really knew the art of training, and also what judges were looking for in the arena. He also had enough trophies, belt buckles and saddles to fill a room.

Larry trained me as well as my horse. We won the 1993 ABRA (American Buckskin Registry Association) World Championship, with my junior horse (a horse under 5 years old), a beautiful buckskin mare he had bred on his ranch and raised, named, "Ima A Smokin' Janie", and in 1994 we took Reserve World Champion. The 1994 event was special for me because I got to compete against a legend in the cutting horse arena, an inductee in the NCHA Hall of Fame and a true cowboy – Matlock Rose. I won that time.

There's a season for everything, including riding in competition and taking care of cattle and horses day and night and our season at the ranch came to an end in 2001. We sold the ranch, kept two of our favorite horses, which we moved to a friends place closer to town, and moved to Shawnee, Kansas, a close-in suburb of Kansas City.

As of this writing in 2005, we still see our horses everyday and give them their nightly treats, but someone else does the feeding and turning out and makes sure their hooves are trimmed.

The memories are there, and I still love the smell of fresh hay, horses and leather.

The Heart in Communicating

CHAPTER 21

"The Winning Game Plan"

I began to concentrate solely on teaching my seminar, which by this time was taking me somewhere in the country at least 3 times a month. My calendar was often booked 10 months in advance.

As I mentioned earlier, video production was being replaced by newer technology, and I was fine with that. Often when I would drive around Kansas City, I would remark to Susan, how many of these buildings I had hauled video production gear in and out of over the years.

And, now when flying in and out of airports around the country, I'm very content to be carrying my small briefcase with seminar notes instead of a 35 pound television camera and all the other associated production gear.

In 2004, after Auburn had won the Sugar Bowl, I received a call from Meredith Jenkins, the University's Associate Athletic Director, and another friend, Deedie Dowdle, the University's Communications Director. They asked if I would come down to Auburn and present my seminar on "Risk Communications and Media Response Training" to the new Athletic Director and members of the University staff.

Meredith also asked if I would also be willing to spend some time with the football team as they were getting a lot of media attention in the wake of their undefeated season and Sugar Bowl win. Of course I said yes. But, then I got to thinking, what do I say to a room full of 18-year-old athletes?

The session with them was held in the sports amphitheater, and as they entered the room with a member of the coaching staff standing at each door, I could hear some of them saying, "We have to be here how long – two hours?"

"I don't like the media".

"Who's this guy anyway?"

I had the feeling I was walking uphill in a mudslide before getting started. My first thoughts were, "How am I going to motivate these guys to want to learn about responding to the media in the first place; and how can I describe it in a way that would be meaningful to them in their present mindset?"

The Bridging Chart. It looks just like a football field! I told them they played and practiced everyday on a large football field, but when the media comes to interview them, they're playing on a ping-pong table. You simply can't play football on a ping-pong table! I said, "Let me show you the winning play for next year's 'Media Bowl' game. If you can master this play, you'll win the 'Media Bowl'." I was beginning to get their attention.

I then drew the diagram of what news looks like. The bad news on the left and the good news on the right. (See the diagram below.) I had them draw this diagram with me as I used the large coaches dry-erase board in the front of the amphitheater. This is also what I call the Bridging Chart.

1	Bridging Chart	1
2		2
3		3
4		4
5		5
6		6
7		7
8		8
9		9
10		10

I had them number 1 through 10 on the bad (left) side, which represented their 10 worst situations, that if they happened, and if they improperly responded to them, would leave a negative impact on the team and Auburn.

Then, on the right side, I had them do the same. Place 10 numbers that represented the good things that Auburn Football represents, and we would call them "themes". These themes would tell the rest of the story.

Now the diagram really started looking not only like a football field, but the check marks representing the opposing players became quite clear.

Here's the formula, I told them - the winning play. I told them I wanted them to answer the reporters question in 4 seconds, and to make sure they answered it honestly. If they didn't, the remaining part of their answer would have no credibility.

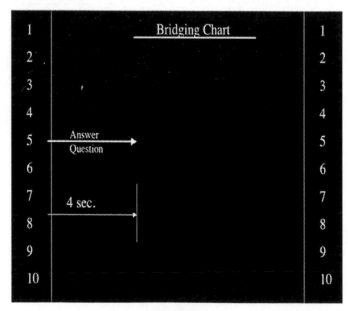

Then, use the reporter's first name or some phrase that acts as a "bridge", such as, "As I said before Mary"......"John, and equally important here", etc. The bridge acts as both a physical and mental reminder that you must use two themes in each response.

Then, state your first theme. Remember, the time limit is four seconds.

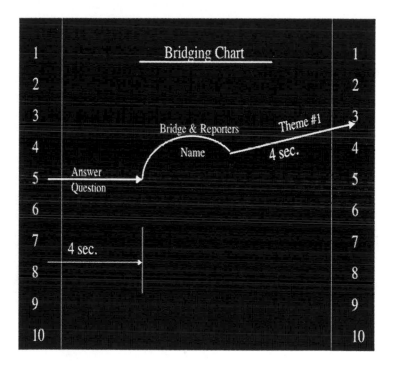

Then state your second theme - again in four seconds.

After you've said your two main points, the themes that you want your audience to hear, <u>stop</u>. Both of your themes must be no longer than 4 seconds each.

There's your 12-second sound bite. And, it can't be edited! You just insured that you wouldn't be taken out of context.

Remember, you must repeat the two themes in every response. The response you leave the two themes out of is probably the one that will get aired. Why? Simple. You stayed with the reporter's agenda and failed to provide balance and perspective to the story.

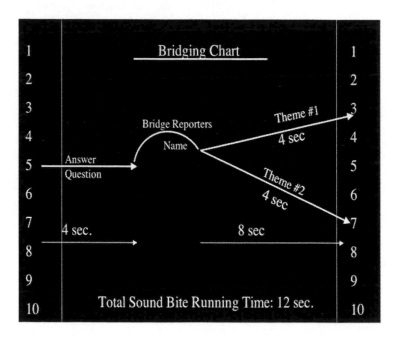

Look at the diagram again. The left side, the first four seconds — your answer to each different question — will be different, because it's a different question being asked. *But, your two themes will be the same.*

Answer the new question and then bridge to your themes <u>again</u> by saying, "and, John, once again the most important things, etc., etc."

The team got it! One of the most gratifying things a teacher can receive is to have an 18 year old come up afterwards and say, "Man that was cool!" "Neat stuff".

With adult education, people attend with expectations. With kids, you have to prove you care about them before they open up to learn.

I left that day with a Sugar Bowl coach's hat signed by Auburn's head coach Tommy Tuberville, inscribed, "Thanks Dick, War Eagle!"

CHAPTER 22

"Doppler Radiation"

*W*hat are themes, and how do they relate to the story? How important are they and how do you develop them? Let me give you an example, and then show you how you can practice with staff members in your own organization.

About 8 times a year, I go to the National Weather Service's National Training Center in Kansas City and teach meteorologists from around the world who come there for training. I teach them how to respond to the media after natural disasters such as hurricanes, tornados, tsunamis or other natural crisis events.

These people are scientists. To them those are not clouds; those are "altocumulonimbus stratus-lenticularis". To you and I that's a thundercloud. But, we all have our professional jargon. To doctors, it could be the intervertebral fibrous cartilaginous disk. A disk in the back.

I had passed out a different case study to each table of the meteorologists in this particular seminar, and there were about 8 tables, with 5 students per table. After they reviewed their case studies and developed their two themes that I talked about previously, I would call on someone from each table to come up and I'd do an "on-camera" interview, followed by a playback and critique.

This particular table got a case study that centered around the large Doppler radar that we've all seen around the country - the large white domes that resemble a giant golf ball on stilts.

I had created a situation where homeowners in a subdivision were complaining about this radar being so close to their homes. They were worried about the radiation from it, and also the fact that some felt it was driving down the resale value of their homes.

Well, when the tables began reading their case studies, this particular table let out several gasps. It seems that the case study I had created had actually happened in a suburb of Los Angeles, where the actor who played "J.R." in Dallas, Larry Hagman lived. At the time I think he also had a lawsuit against the National Weather Service about this very same thing.

I selected a meteorologist from that table to come up for an interview, and it started easily enough with some simple questions like, "How many of these Doppler radar's do you have around the country? "Do they give you more warning time in case of severe weather?"

And, he answered them easily and without an undue amount of nervousness, until I asked him, "How many innocent victims are you poisoning with radiation from this radar?

At that point, his body language changed entirely. He went back into his "box", his safety zone, and reverted to professional jargon that I could not understand at all. Something like, "Well, the M-88D, Doppler Radar bisects the polarity of the altocumulonimbus stratus lenticularis...."

I stopped the interview, sent the cameraman away and said, "Let's pretend that I'm your son, and I'm 10 years old and just came home from school, ok? "Dad, the kids at school are saying that you're hurting them with your radar - are you?"

He looked right at me - made the transition from the professional "box", to one of parental concern, and said,

"Absolutely not. The radar listens most of the time and gives off less energy than a cell phone... (4 second answer).....

"But, Dick, for the first time....(bridge)...

"we can 'see' inside of the cloud and can see that hook signature that tells us a tornado's coming...(4 second theme number one)....

and that gives us more warning time than we've ever had, and let's me do my mission to protect lives and property"....(4 second theme number two)

A perfect 12-second sound bite! In thinking for a moment that he was actually talking to his son, he simply said what he felt. (Go back and look again at the completed bridging chart and apply his answers to that chart. See how they match exactly?)

I have interviewed literally thousands of people and I can physically see when someone is responding from their head or their heart. The body language signs are very specific. More on that later.

CHAPTER 23

"The Breakdown"

*T*he breakdown I'm going to show you is really the "macro" view of where you fit into a news story. You've already seen the "micro" view in the soundbite graphs. Now, let's look at where that soundbite fits into the overall story. A story that may only run 50 seconds on the evening news.

Most will agree that newspapers generate a lead within the inverted pyramid format. The lead is at the top and contains the who, what, where, when and why in the first few lines.

This was originally done during the days when news came over the telegraph lines, which were prone to going down quickly and often. So, the telegraphers learned to put the most important facts of the story in what they called the lead.

Today, that practice is still used, and gives editors the opportunity cut the story almost anywhere and still retain the most important facts about the item.

In a television news story, I think the shape is more like an hourglass.

There still is the lead, or the open, which is usually a wide shot of some scene, followed by what I call the story development. This is usually a closer shot of the action.

Next comes the introduction to the soundbite.

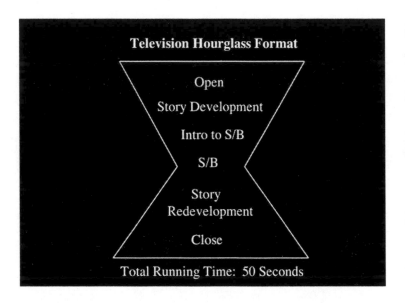

Remember, that's where the person who is going to be interviewed is introduced to the viewer. The viewer can't go back and "re-hear" the soundbite, so they must be prepared for who this person is, his or her title, and why the person's important to the story. This is usually a medium close up shot.

Next is the all-important soundbite. You've already seen the graphics on this critical element. This is a close up shot.

Do you see how the hourglass is being formed, from the wide shot in the beginning to the close up shot for the soundbite?

After the soundbite comes a medium wide shot that I call story redevelopment. This can be a sidebar issue or other facts about the story that help to develop it.

And, then there is the close, which is usually done in about the same location as the opening standup, and is a wider shot showing the same amount of action as the opening sequence.

Here is a graphic showing the basic elements of a news story for television and the running times associated with it.

News Story Breakdown

1. "Stand Up" Open:	Running Time: 00:08
2. Story Development:	Running Time: 00:07
3. Intro to Interview:	Running Time: 00:06
4. "Sound Bite":	Running Time: 00.12
5. Story Re-development:	Running Time: 00:07
6. "Stand Up" Close:	Running Time: 00:08
	Total Running Time: 00:50

Let's develop a television report about a flood and see if you can read the story and relate it back to the News Story Breakdown Chart.

Open: (Wide Shot) Reporter standing on bank of river. Camera is pointing at reporter and in the background across the swollen river we see emergency vehicle lights and activity in the small village on the other side.) *Reporter: "Perhaps nowhere along this fifteen hundred mile stretch of the Missouri River is a town more threatened than the historic town of Riverside."*

Story Development: (Medium Shot) Reporter and crew go across the river and are standing on the edge of main street with the flashing emergency lights on vehicles and activity in the background. The reporter is off camera. *Reporter: "Hundreds of volunteers as well as those who live here are engaged in a desperate attempt to shore up the aging dike before flood waters crest tonight at 12 feet above flood stage."*

Introduction to the Soundbite: (Medium Close Up) Remember, in an electronic interview we have to identify who the person is, his or her title and why they are important to the story. Reporter is off camera. *Reporter: "Also here as part of this desperate attempt to save this town is Brigadier General John Smith and more than 150 Missouri National Guardsmen from the 149 Engineer Battalion."*

Now we know who is going to be interviewed, what his title is, and how many men he is commanding and where they are from. We know quite a bit about this person who is yet to speak. And, we've gone one step further. We've made up our minds whether or not we like him just by looking at his body language.

Soundbite: (Close Up) Next is the all-important soundbite. The General speaks hope-fully with authority and compassion what his troops are doing as citizen soldiers who live and work her also.

Story Redevelopment: (Medium Wide Shot) Now the hourglass starts to widen out again. Again the reporter is off camera. *Reporter: "In addition to the Army Guardsmen, and those who live and work here, there are more than 50 Red Cross volunteers passing out blankets and food stuffs to those who have been displaced by this historic flood."*

Close: (Wide Shot) Now the on camera close to the story showing river and reporter) The reporter is again on the other side of the river near the spot where the crew did the open. *Reporter: "Even if the dike somehow holds tonight, it will be a long time before residents and business owners return to this flood ravaged community. From the banks of the Missouri River at Riverside, I'm Richard Brundage, reporting."*

CHAPTER 24

"Practice Makes Perfect"

*Y*ou've already studied the diagram of what a sound-bite looks like in previous chapters, so let's talk about how you practice it.

I told you to place check marks on the left side of the news diagram that represent your 10 worst nightmares. Those are the things that if they happened, and if you improperly responded to them would leave a negative impact on your organization.

And, on the right side, you've made an equal number of check marks that represent things that you do better than anyone else. Themes that tell the rest of the story.

At the end of your scheduled weekly or monthly meetings, bring up one of those nightmare situations, and have your management team develop two themes that tell the rest of the story. The first time they write those themes, they'll do so silently. Now, ask them to say it out loud.

My guess is, from the hundreds of seminars I've conducted, they will sound like they're reading from a well-scripted page. Perfect English, and a long compound, complex sentence. Certainly not one you would actually say out loud. It's like trying to read aloud the lead in a newspaper story. The newspaper is written for the eye, and your themes should be written for the ear. Each four seconds long.

In broadcasting we wanted to know what the words sounded like. Certainly we wanted to use good grammar, but we wrote in all CAPS so that we could read it on a teleprompter, and used ..... for pauses or emphasis. The most important thing was to make sure the viewer and listener would take away the essence of the story the first time.

Your theme development should have the same mission. Keep shortening it, using simpler words and everyday language, and most importantly complete each theme in no more than 4 seconds.

Then, and only after you've refined each of those themes to 4 seconds each and agreed on them as a group, can you now approach the second step. Practice.

Select a spokesperson at the table. The rest of you are now playing the role of reporters. Ask your spokesperson a question. (And, remember, you will always know more about the story than the reporter, so ask tough questions. Anyone can answer the easy ones.)

The spokesperson should answer your question, use your name, and bridge to the two themes. All in 12 seconds. Someone at the table should be the "timer". If the spokesperson goes over 12 seconds, cut him or her off.

Ask another question. Remember, the first part, the 4-second answer to the questions will always be different won't it? It's a different question. *But, the two themes remain the same.* Simply answer the question and bridge to those two themes. The media is only going to air one response. That's all the time there is. Don't deliver a soundbite *without* 2 themes.

You can also practice this one day a week while driving to work. (I recommend you wear a cellular mic at your face so other drivers don't think you're talking to yourself – or maybe you're comfortable with that image?)

While driving, take a crisis situation that you've already developed 2 themes for and ask yourself the questions. Answer the question, use someone's name, and bridge to those two 4 second themes. Do this for 15 minutes once a week driving to work and watch how fast you learn to talk in credible and honest soundbites!

It's a skill that requires practice. It's very much like learning to play the piano, or golf. The first time you try these things it's awkward, and there is so much to learn and remember. But, after you've practiced, you develop what I call "The Three M's" - *Mental Muscle Memory.*

Pretty soon, you don't have to remember the 12 things in a backswing; you just enjoy playing the game of golf. I never want my students to have to think about what they are going to say. I want them to already know *what* they are going to say and then concentrate on *performing* it!

One final thought that rounds out the development of themes for each crisis situation. For each check mark you made on the left side of the bridging chart that signified a potential crisis situation, make a one-page fact sheet.

For instance, if one of your crises is "tornados", make a one-page fact sheet that you can give the reporter about tornados. The fact sheet should be done in bullet point style.

For example:

FACT SHEET - TORNADOS

- Approximately 900 tornados touch down in the U.S. each year.

- The U.S. has more tornados than any continent in the world.

- Tornados are measured on the "Fujita Scale" from 0 to 5, which is a measurement of wind speed.

- The largest outbreak of tornados occurred, etc.

You get the point. Whenever a person hands a fact sheet to a reporter in the pre-interview, the reporter can always go back to the station and verify the facts on the sheet, but they don't have to re-invent the wheel by doing a lot of research to get the same facts you just gave them.

The result is simply this. If you give the reporter facts and not fluff, you are likely to hear some of that information come back in the story being aired that night.

So, now you are not only getting your 12 second sound bite on the air, and saying it the way you want using the bridging chart format, you'll be getting additional facts being aired as well.

The reporter is very apt to lead into your soundbite with some the facts that you provided, and end with some as well.

Each potential crisis should have a fact sheet, and two themes that tell the rest of the story and put it into perspective.

In your crisis communications plan do this. On page one, place the crisis. Write a paragraph or two about some critical situation that could happen. On page two, write two themes that tell the rest of the story. On page three, create a fact sheet with bullet items about that kind of event.

Do that with all of your potential crisis events and place them in your crisis communications plan. And then practice them with your staff. By the end of the year you will have covered virtually all of your potential crisis events. You will be prepared to communicate.

CHAPTER 25

"The Pre-Interview"

*D*oing a "pre-interview" with the reporter is an absolute. There should be no such thing as an "ambush interview". No reporter has a God-given right to an instantaneous interview! And, you should never grant one.

Let's say you're an educator. All day long you've been thinking about and practicing your profession, education. About 2 O'clock in the afternoon, a reporter stops you as you're going from one building on the campus to the next, and wants an interview. He has a camera crew with him. What do you do? Say, "No comment". Of course not.

First of all, you *want* to do the interview, reaching perhaps a million people that night with your message, but you also want to perform it right, and put it in the correct soundbite format. You can't do that on the spur of the moment – no one can. You simply need a little time.

Tell the reporter, "Of course, I'll to talk with you. Let's go to my office." Never let the reporter dictate where the interview is going to be held. Remember, when a reporter and camera crew show up wanting an interview – they belong to you. If you're comfortable doing your interview sitting on the corner of your desk with your diplomas in the background, fine. If you're comfortable standing by the door with the seal of your institution on it, do it there. You decide.

There are several basics steps you should take in any encounter with the media.

First of all – introduce yourself to everyone in the crew. And, I think I'd start with the cameraperson. That's the person who control 87% of the story – the visuals – you. The entire crew is important.

Second, ask the obvious: "What story are you working on today?" Logical, yes. Often asked, no. Sometimes people walk right into an interview knowing almost nothing about the subject. I find that incredible!

Nothing may be happening in your school district today, but something happened elsewhere, and perhaps this reporter is trying to localize a national story.

I don't think there was a superintendent of a major school district in this country, on the first anniversary of the shootings at Columbine, who wasn't interviewed by some reporter asking, "What have you done to make your school district safer this year?" Their school district was probably safe already.

Third, find out who else is going to be in the story with you that evening. Are members of your Board of Education going to be interviewed also?

Fourth, locate the cameraperson. This is the person in the crew that has the most to carry, and takes the longest amount of time to set up. Just ignore the cameraperson and you've effectively jeopardized 87% of your story already. Tell the cameraperson where you're going to be doing the interview and have them go there and set up while you're doing a pre-interview with the reporter.

Now you have the cameraperson out of the room and on the way to the interview location to get set up. Now you can talk with the reporter. You know the subject, and it's likely about one of the check marks on the left side of your bridging chart that you developed earlier – a crisis event. If that's the case, you have already developed the two themes as well as the fact sheet.

Find out what story angle the reporter is developing, and also if there is any specific information that he or she is looking for that you might be able to provide for them. Act as a resource. Remember, at this point, this is your story now, not theirs.

If you would like to have a reporter ask you a certain question, you might say, "You know the question I'm most often asked about this subject", and then state the question. I can almost guarantee you'll hear that question come back to you during the interview. There isn't a reporter alive who wants to miss "the question most often asked".

Then, excuse yourself for a few minutes by saying, "By the time Bob gets the camera equipment set up, I'll be back. Give me about 10 minutes to get the information and facts together that you'll need for your story." Be honest. The reporter has been thinking about this story since the 10 0'clock meeting that morning at the station, when all of the producers, reporters and camera people gather to determine what stories are going to be covered, and who's going to do them. You have been doing school administration things.

Get your management team together. The same people you developed the bridging chart with. The same people who wrote a paragraph on each crisis event and developed the themes for each as well as the fact sheets.

Tell them why the reporter is here today, and refresh your memory about the two themes. Re-institute "Mental Muscle Memory".

Think of it as an athletic event. Do you think Tiger Woods would tee off in a major tournament without first hitting several hundred balls with each club in his bag? Or maybe a marathon runner might stretch the ham-strings a little, or a piano player run the keyboard a few times loosening up the fingers and going over a difficult part of the score?

The same applies for the mind, the body and the face. Have your staff ask you tough questions about the issue, and you answer them, using the questioner's name and then bridge to the two themes and stop. Let each of your management team ask you difficult questions, and answer each and bridge to those themes.

If you do this for just 10 minutes, you'll find your mental muscle memory returning, and you once again know what you're going to say. Now, you can *concentrate on how you're saying something*. You should never have to think about what you're going to say – you already know that. Just perform it.

Now, you're ready to go meet the reporter in the location you chose for your interview and take charge. If you do this – in the sequence above – you'll be amazed at the results when you watch yourself on the evening news.

I remember asking Dr. Fred Rogers, following his keynote address to the American Academy of Pediatricians in Dallas, if I could have a separate interview with him. He did exactly what I've just described to you. He said, "Of course. Here's the key to my suite. Why don't you and crew get set up? I'll be up there in about 10 minutes, ok?"

The crew and I went up to the suite. There were about 6 people in the crew. We lit the area he had mentioned, and I placed the camera low on the tripod so that we could conduct the interview on the couch. We had the microphones and cables all laid out for the anchor and Mr. Rogers, when he walked in.

He entered the room and proceeded to introduce himself to everyone in the crew, starting with the soundman, the make up person, and the video engineer, all the way around the room. It only took about 60 seconds, but he made everyone feel important. He didn't have to do that. He was a star.

We got him situated on the couch, along with the anchor and clipped both of their mic's on. I was standing behind the camera with my ear-phones on, and said, "Mr. Rogers, would you mind saying a few words so that I can set your audio level?"

He looked up at me and said, "Dick, it's nice to be in your 'neighborhood'.

Well, he could have said anything after that, and it would have been all right with me. The interview went great, and his soundbite was of course succinct, heartfelt and aired that way. The way he wanted it to.

The point here is that you are in control of the total interview, and perhaps no one has ever told you that before. It's your interview. Without you, they don't really have a story. They need someone in the story with a soundbite to give it that human element. You're that person.

Follow those simple steps in the pre-interview, and be amazed at the results!

CHAPTER 26

"Heart Surgery"

*T*here are 44 muscles in the face, and unlike all other muscles in the body that are connected to bones by ligaments and tendons, these 44 muscles are 'free-floating'.

Someone recently did a study on how many emotions the human face is capable of showing. I found the results staggering! I knew there was a full range of emotions that were complex and numerous. But, not 5,000! That's what this study concluded.

We're all experts at body language, but perhaps no one has put academic handles on some of them for you. What can you see on someone's face at 100 feet? The most common answer I hear is "an attitude". That's probably right. How were you able to ascertain that? Body language. And, almost all of it came from the face.

When you're on television, you can discard taste, touch and smell - 3 of the 5 primary senses. You only have seeing and hearing left. As I mentioned before, seeing is 87%. Hearing is only 7%. It literally doesn't make any difference what you say on television, it's how you say it that matters.

Often we say things before we open our mouths just through our body language. How many times have you been doing something else around the house but had the TV on, and there is "60-Minutes" or some other investigative program, and they are introducing someone prior to that person speaking. All you see is that person's face while the reporter is giving that person's name and credentials.

You've already made several decisions simply by looking at that person's face. You've decided whether or not you like that person, and consequently the credibility of that person before they speak. We've all, a one time or another, looked at someone being introduced, and said to ourselves - or out loud - "guilty". Be an active and pleasant listener with your face.

Back in the late 90's, I was conducting a one-on-one consultation with a noted heart surgeon who had just written a book and was scheduled to be on the "Today Show".

He wanted some training on how to appear and how he should say certain things. I knew that he would probably have no more than 3 minutes to talk and interact with the morning show hosts, so I was simply shortening down his sound bites.

But, what struck me the most was this doctor's incredible enthusiasm for life in general and his outgoing passion for his profession.

Heart surgeons aren't generally known for their effervescent personalities. It takes 4 years of college, 4 years of medical school, more years of intern and residencies, and perhaps 10 years after medical school you become a heart surgeon.

Imagine the dedication and laser focus it must take. And, each year they pursue this dream, they become more detached from the rest of us. They find they have fewer people to talk to, to interact with. They sometimes find themselves alone in rarified air.

Not this surgeon. He was absolutely wonderful to talk with. When I got done with the coaching part of the consultation, I asked him, "Where did you learn to do this - to be so outgoing and passionate about your career?"

He looked at me with one of the most compassionate faces I've ever seen, and said, "Oh, I learned what a heart surgeon was all about when I woke up in intensive care after they'd cracked my chest and done a triple by-pass. At that moment I became a heart surgeon. I'll never forget the recovery room nurse holding my hand. A simple gesture, but it brought humanity to the theater.

Now, I never go to one of my patient's room before or after surgery and say something like, 'How are we today'? One of us isn't fine, and it's probably my patient! I'll always touch them, sometimes I'll sit on the bed with them, hold their hands, and sometimes I'll even cry with them.

It's literally changed the way I practice medicine. And, you know what? My patients heal faster."

The lesson for me there was that nothing takes the place of human touch and compassion. I always tell my students to reach out and touch the audience with their words, and never be afraid to show emotion. Emotions are so visible in the face, and contrary to popular belief, the most powerful person on television is the one who is perceived to be the most vulnerable.

It's almost the opposite of what happens around a corporate boardroom table. First of all, the position of the people at the table gives the power structure away immediately.

Secondly, the CEO of any large corporation didn't necessarily get to be the CEO by being open and vulnerable. I suspect it's quite the opposite in some cases. But the open and honest person – it's powerful.

CHAPTER 27

"Talking to the Child"

*L*ook in a mirror and talk about a current story that is making news. Talk to an adult. Now do the same exercise and talk to a child in the mirror. Watch the amazing difference!

Talk to someone you love. Wonderful things happen to your face and your body language. I always imagine I'm talking to my two daughters and when I do, my face lights up, my sentences are shorter and my language very direct and simple - and pleasant.

Why do we do that as parents? For one reason only. We want our children to understand and appreciate what we are saying. What is the difference with our audience? Isn't it exactly the same?

We've all been taught - particularly men - to mask emotions. "Cowboy up." "Don't wear your heart on your sleeve." "Keep a poker face.", etc.

What a mistake! By the time we've grown up our ability to show real emotion about many things is virtually gone. You can, however, get it back. It's still there, just hidden.

When you're being interviewed and you look at the reporter and respond to the reporter, that's where your message stops. The reporter is only the 'gatekeeper' of your message. He or she has the ability to distort your message, but not if you talk in sound bites, and if you relate to your audience - not the reporter.

Stop talking *to* the reporter. I want you to look directly at the reporter when you respond, but I want you to focus just beyond the reporter and concentrate on someone you love. Respond to that person. Talk *through* the reporter to a target audience you want to reach. Watch what happens to your face, your voice and the brevity and clarity of your responses. You will be amazed.

We mirror the face and often the body language of the person we're talking to. Often reporters may have a frown on their faces, or are not looking at you at all, but writing notes. Your face will mirror this action.

Instead, talk to the "child". It's amazing how clear our sentences become, how understandable the complex issues are, and how memorable the response will be if you forget you're talking to an adult.

I had come to a natural break in my seminar for a group of Public Health doctors and nurses at their annual training convention. A woman approached and introduced herself, told me her name and that she was a surgical nurse.

She had just listened to my story about the heart surgeon and said that she had a story she wanted to tell me in the hopes that I would take it and tell my future students. I was so moved by the story, that not only do I include it in all of my seminars, I also wanted to write about it in this book.

She told me that when her daughter was just 3 months old, she needed open-heart surgery to correct some problem. As you can imagine, she said, there are few pediatric heart surgeons capable of operating on a heart that small.

As she was still nursing the baby, her cot was situated right next to the baby's hospital bed. A curtain was drawn around the baby's bed.

The night before the operation, at about 3:30 in the morning, a soft light came on over the baby's crib, and the mother could hear someone softly talking and see the shadow of someone's back behind the curtain, and a hand gently stroking the baby's head.

She thought it was a nurse making middle of the night rounds, but the soft talking went on for several minutes. Not wanting to interrupt, she sat up from her cot, and quietly pulled the curtain back just enough to see the back of the person doing the talking. It was the surgeon! He was leaning over the crib in his scrubs, talking to the baby and stroking her forehead.

He was quietly telling this baby how he was going to take such good care of her that day, and that she was going to run and play with the other kids and would never remember this at all, and not to worry about a thing. Everything he had learned was just for her today.

She let the curtain go back in place, and laid back down on her cot with tears in her eyes. She told me she felt like she was interrupting a very intimate conversation between two people, but most importantly - she also knew at that moment she had the right surgeon!

I'm always moved by that story. The surgeon didn't need to do that. But, that was "real" communications. And, at some level, the baby knew that this was a good person, and the surgeon took time to know his patient, and the family left the hospital with a successful outcome and a wonderful story about "communicating from the heart".

I tell all my medical seminar participants, everyone who comes into your hospital leaves with a story. It's not about how wonderful your new equipment was, or your new techniques. It's about people and how they were treated. How hospital personnel communicated with them. When people come into a hospital they are probably not feeling good, and they are scared. At that moment nothing is more effective or appreciated than good communications and compassion.

CHAPTER 28

"Final Tidbits"

*H*ere are a few random tidbits of information that just didn't seem to fit anywhere else in the book, but I thought important enough to be included here.

1. Sun in your eyes: Here's a trick to help you keep from squinting when you are facing the sun doing an interview on-camera. I used to do this whenever I had to do a standup outdoors.

With your eyes closed, tilt your head back so that your face is directly towards the sun. Your pupils will constrict behind your closed eyelids. Do this for about 10 seconds and then looking straight ahead at the reporter you'll be able to do your interview without squinting. Your pupils should stay constricted for several minutes.

2. Where do you look? Always look directly at the person interviewing you. The psychology here is that the audience (the camera) is usually slightly off center and would rather be an observer to an event. When you look at the camera you are making the audience a participant. Forget the camera.

3. Record your interviews: As a policy, I tell all of my clients to record their interviews. The media is, and you should have a record of exactly what you said in response to each question. It also serves to keep the reporter honest. Subliminally, you're saying, "Don't take me too far out of context. I've got a recording too." You should keep all of your interviews as a record.

4. What if the reporter asks the same question again? I can only think of one reason why a reporter would ask the same question again. He or she didn't get the answer they were looking for! Your first answer is usually the best. I think it's best to simply say, "I think I've answered that, do you have anything else?" First of all that statement won't get aired, and secondly you've just put the reporter on notice - don't go there anymore, I've given you my best answer.

5. What if you get your 'tang all toungled up? Remember, its only going into the recorder on the camera. Just say, "Listen, I can give you a better sound-bite than that…..I think your question was"….. (repeat the question) and then pause for an edit point, and give your answer again.

It's your interview, not the reporter's. Besides, as reporters, we owned the edit gear, so we could do as many stand-up's as we needed until *we* got it right. It's patently unfair to think that you, the person being interviewed, is only going to have one shot at it. That's part of controlling the interview.

Watch a different channel every night: You can certainly learn reporter's styles in your home viewing area by watching different channels for their news programs. Does a certain channel have a "beat" reporter that would cover "news" events in your professional area?

6. Never go "off the record". I tell all my clients, "If you don't want to see it on the evening news, don't say it". I don't know how many reporters today know the difference between, "off the record, "on background", "not for attribution". But, don't take a chance. You've seen it happen many times before, and the person says, "I thought we were off the record."

7. Practice with a mirror: Get a remote control in one hand, and a mirror in the other. Watch one news story, hit the mute button on the remote, turn into the mirror and tell the mirror that story without talking. Just use your facial expressions. Great exercise for getting used to using facial expressions when you talk – on camera or not.

8. The 6 C's of Broadcast Journalism: If professional journalists apply them, so should we in our responses. When I taught Broadcast Journalism at the Defense Information School several summers when I was in the Army Reserves, I told my students to make sure their stories contained the six "C's": Correct, Complete, Current, Concise, Clear, and Conversational. Do the same when you write your responses or "news releases".

9. The "Pregnant Pause". Don't get caught up in it. When you stop talking and the reporter simply stands there with the microphone, don't feel it's your job to fill "dead airtime". It's not. It's the reporter's job to keep the interview going. But, I've seen countless executives, uneasy with three seconds of dead air, attempt to fill that time and blurt out some nonsense that makes the air that evening.

10. Be confident in your knowledge: Remember, you will always know more about the story than the reporter. That's why they're coming to you. Be confident that you have the latest and most complete information about the subject at hand.

11. Don't try to answer a question you don't understand! I don't know why this happens, but we've all seen someone try to answer a question that they don't understand. Simply ask the reporter to either repeat the question or state it in another way so that you can give them the correct answer. They're not going to air that. And, it gives you a little time to think about the appropriate answer.

12. Make Up: If you are going to a television studio, you are going to need make up, and they don't have make up people on staff anymore. Simply go through the cosmetic section at your anchor store in the mall and ask the sales lady what shade of powder you need to match your skin. Reporters use compacts and so should you. It simply removes the oil that shines under the studio lights, and believe me the lights are bright. Anything that detracts from a great appearance, try to fix it before going on the air.

FINAL THOUGHTS

11/17/2005

A lot has happened since my "First Thoughts of 2002". Many more seminars have been conducted around the world, from Prague, Helsinki, Budapest, Guam, Mexico, Saipan, and a host of seminars on the mainland U.S.

My decision to finish the book was helped along and my thanks to Peter Callaghan, a rather extraordinary fellow, author, Press Secretary for the Governor of Saipan, and my friend.

In March of 2005, I presented my seminar on Guam, and Pete had flown in from Saipan to attend. We immediately struck up a friendship and had conversations during the breaks in my seminar there that day.

We discovered throughout the day that we both had Vietnam experience, he in the Air Force, shot down in an F4 Phantom jet and a prisoner of war, and I, in the Army, with two combat tours in Vietnam at about the same time.

He, too, wrote a book, and we talked not about the importance of getting published, but the mental catharsis of just getting it down on paper.

Both of us had written on different subjects, but nevertheless the desire to write was a driving force, even if the end result would only be memoirs for our children.

Pete was impressed with the seminar, enough to insist that I come to Saipan and present it later in the year. He also said that if I wanted to stay for several more weeks on Saipan, I'd find it the perfect spot for writing. He and I both knew I'd probably never get it done in Kansas City with all the distractions, cell phones, emails, etc.

He was right. As I write these final thoughts now, I'm sitting in a perfect location on the beautiful island of Saipan, surrounded by quiet, palm trees and the Pacific Ocean where thoughts can flow much like the natural order of things here. Pete also did my initial editing, offering many suggestions that really made this book better. Thanks Pete.

As of this writing, I'm a mere 4 weeks away from being 65. Social Security, Medicare and the realities of life don't merely lurk in the shadows, they stampede openly into my daily life. For the first time, I'm acutely aware of things like longevity, actuarial tables, and give more thought to the minor aches and pains that in youth were simple inconveniences, gone the next day.

All of this, and knowing that I'm in the absolute prime of my teaching career, makes this book even more important to me. I may have further successes in teaching around the world, but *nothing* will begin to compare to what is past.

And, perhaps, for a future generation of Brundages, this compendium of thoughts, written as milestones in my life, will be a brief history about one life, most of the time lived like everyone else - in quiet desperation, wondering what was around the next bend in the road, anxious to see what it was, and often amazed at the events that unfolded.

Above all, remember this:

Words are sacred. They deserve respect. If you pick the right ones, and put them in the right order, you can nudge the world a little.

Go ahead, nudge the world – it needs it.

Thank you all for making my glass in life more than half full. You have enriched me beyond anything I could have possibly imagined, and no matter how much I give back, it will never equal the amount given by you.

God Bless you all.

Richard Wm. Brundage
November, 2005
Saipan, CNM

Jacket Design: Tara Brundage

Visit our website: www.mediatrainers.com

If you would like to schedule Richard for a live seminar for your organization, please contact him at:

Richard Brundage, President
Center for Advanced Media Studies
P.O. Box 12266
Overland Park, KS 66282

Or, call his personal cell phone: 913-927-1777

Or, Email: RBrundage@earthlink.net

Website: www.mediatrainers.com

From medical, corporate, legal and educational professionals to government, association executives, and industry leaders, Brundage has trained some of the world's top executives with his insightful, intensive and practical techniques.

His uniquely supportive workshops yield immediate and lasting results for all who participate.

He was recently selected by the State Department to train new U.S. Ambassadors, and in 2001, was the only crisis communicator in North America to be featured in the 60-minute television special, "Global Risk Management".